THE COMPLETE ITALIAN COOKBOOK

1000 Days of Sophisticated and Elegant Italian Recipes to Enrich Your Culinary Repertoire

Sharron B. Malec

Editor: Aaliyah Lyons

Cover Art: Danielle Rees

Interior Design: Brooke White

Food stylist: Sienna Adams

TABLE OF CONTENTS

TABLE OF CONTENTS

TABLE OF CONTENTS

INTRODUCTION

Italian cuisine, with its centuries-old culinary traditions, rich tapestry of regional flavors, and unwavering commitment to fresh, high-quality ingredients, is a gastronomic journey like no other. From the charming trattorias of Rome to the bustling pizzerias of Naples and the rustic kitchens of Tuscany, Italian food has woven its way into the hearts and palates of people worldwide.

The roots of Italian cuisine delve deep into history, echoing the influences of ancient civilizations that have shaped its character. This enduring culinary heritage is characterized by a profound respect for simplicity and an embrace of locally sourced, seasonal ingredients. Olive oil, garlic, tomatoes, and pasta serve as the foundation for dishes that transcend mere sustenance, becoming works of art that nourish both body and soul.

But Italian cuisine is not a monolithic entity; it is a mosaic of regional diversity. Each part of Italy, from the northern Alps to the sun-soaked islands of the south, boasts its own distinct flavors and culinary treasures. From creamy risottos in Lombardy to the exquisite cheeses of Emilia-Romagna and the fiery passion of Neapolitan pizza, the sheer variety of Italian dishes is a testament to the country's gastronomic wealth.

This cuisine is more than just a collection of recipes; it's a lifestyle. The Mediterranean diet, characterized by its emphasis on fresh fruits and vegetables, olive oil, whole grains, lean protein, and a moderate intake of wine, promotes not only delicious eating but also a healthful and balanced existence.

At the heart of Italian food lies pasta, an art form unto itself. Fresh pasta, crafted by skilled hands or a pasta machine, possesses a tender, melt-in-your-mouth quality that is pure culinary poetry. Dried pasta, an indispensable pantry staple, takes on myriad forms, each one designed to cradle specific sauces and create harmony on the plate.

Sauces in Italian cuisine are a testament to the power of simplicity and the alchemy of flavors. Tomato-based classics like marinara and pomodoro share the stage with indulgent Alfredo and vibrant pesto sauces. These sauces, often paired with a judicious selection of herbs and spices, elevate even the most basic ingredients to culinary stardom.

Italy's love affair with wine is another integral aspect of its dining culture. A diverse range of grape varieties and wine styles caters to every palate, making wine an indispensable companion to the Italian meal. Whether sipping a robust Tuscan red or a delicate Venetian white, the art of wine appreciation is an essential part of the Italian culinary experience.

Italian dining is not merely about food; it's about forging connections and celebrating life's moments. Long, leisurely meals with family and friends, punctuated by laughter and stories, are the cornerstone of Italian social life. The ritual of aperitivo, a pre-dinner drink and snack, sets the stage for conviviality and relaxation.

No Italian meal is complete without a sweet ending. Italian desserts, ranging from the iconic tiramisu to the delicate cannoli and creamy panna cotta, are irresistible delights that linger on the palate. Gelato, the country's beloved ice cream, offers a refreshing and indulgent way to conclude any culinary adventure.

Italian cuisine's universal appeal can be attributed to its simplicity, freshness, and the fundamental joy of sharing good food with loved ones. In this journey through Italian food, we invite you to savor the beauty and taste of Italy, one dish at a time. Join us as we explore the flavors, traditions, and timeless magic of Italian cuisine. Buon appetito!

CHAPTER 1: EMBARKING ON AN ITALIAN CULINARY ODYSSEY

THE CULTURAL SIGNIFICANCE OF ITALIAN CUISINE

Italian cuisine transcends the boundaries of mere sustenance; it is a cultural treasure that embodies the essence of Italy itself. Beyond the tantalizing aromas and flavors, Italian cooking carries a profound historical, social, and emotional significance that is woven into the very fabric of the nation. To truly appreciate the culinary marvel that is Italian cuisine, one must delve into its cultural roots and understand the role it plays in shaping the identity of Italy and its people.

A HISTORICAL TAPESTRY

Italian cuisine's cultural significance is rooted in history, tracing its origins to ancient civilizations. The influences of the Etruscans, Greeks, and Romans have left indelible marks on the ingredients, cooking techniques, and flavors that define Italian food today.

The Romans, in particular, played a pivotal role in shaping the culinary landscape. Their penchant for extravagant banquets and the use of a wide array of ingredients laid the groundwork for the rich diversity of Italian cooking. Ingredients like olive oil, garlic, and wine became staples that continue to feature prominently in Italian cuisine.

However, it was during the Middle Ages that Italian cuisine truly began to take shape. The emergence of city-states, such as Florence, Venice, and Genoa, led to trade and cultural exchange with neighboring regions, further enriching the culinary repertoire. The spice trade, in particular, brought an array of flavors from distant lands to Italian kitchens.

REGIONAL DIVERSITY

Perhaps one of the most striking aspects of Italian cuisine is its regional diversity. Italy's unique geography, with its varied landscapes and climates, has given rise to a vast array of regional cuisines, each with its own distinct flavors and specialties.

From the northern Alpine region to the sun-drenched islands of Sicily and Sardinia, Italy's regional cuisines are a testament to the country's culinary wealth. In the north, the Lombardy region boasts rich, creamy risotto dishes, while Emilia-Romagna is renowned for its handmade pasta and Parmigiano-Reggiano cheese. Tuscany, in central Italy, is celebrated for its hearty soups, robust red wines, and the iconic Florentine steak.

As one journeys south, Naples takes center stage as the birthplace of pizza, a global favorite. The southern regions of Apulia, Calabria, and Campania offer an abundance of fresh seafood, sun-ripened vegetables, and hand-rolled pasta. Sicily, with its unique fusion of flavors influenced by its historical conquerors, has given rise to dishes like arancini (rice balls) and cannoli (sweet pastries).

Each regional cuisine reflects the local terroir, historical influences, and the resourcefulness of its people. It is a testament to Italy's commitment to preserving culinary traditions while embracing innovation.

FAMILY, TRADITION, AND IDENTITY

Italian cuisine is inseparable from the concept of family, tradition, and identity. Meals in Italy are not just about nourishment; they are a cornerstone of social life, a time for families and communities to come together. The act of preparing and sharing food is a means of forging connections and celebrating life's moments.

Italians take immense pride in their culinary heritage, with recipes passed down through generations. Nonnas (grandmothers) and mammas (mothers) are the keepers of family traditions, imparting their wisdom and techniques to the next generation. The importance of preserving these culinary legacies is a testament to the cultural significance of Italian cuisine.

Traditionally, many Italian families have their own gardens, where they grow vegetables, herbs, and even grapes for making wine. This connection to the land is deeply ingrained in the culture, and it's reflected in the emphasis on fresh, locally sourced ingredients. The Italian phrase "km 0" signifies the practice of using ingredients from within a short distance of the home, highlighting the commitment to quality and sustainability.

ARTISTRY IN SIMPLICITY

Italian cuisine's cultural significance also lies in its artistry in simplicity. It is a cuisine that values the intrinsic flavors of ingredients, allowing them to shine with minimal manipulation. The Italians have a saying, "Il piacere della tavola è il piacere della vita» (The pleasure of the table is the pleasure of life), which underscores the importance of savoring each bite.

The Mediterranean diet, of which Italian cuisine is a shining example, emphasizes fresh fruits and vegetables, olive oil, whole grains, lean protein, and a moderate intake of wine. This dietary pattern is not just a matter of health but also a way of life, promoting well-being and longevity.

A GLOBAL AMBASSADOR

Italian cuisine's cultural significance extends far beyond Italy's borders. It has become a global ambassador for the country, introducing people around the world to its flavors and traditions. Italian restaurants can be found in nearly every corner of the globe, serving as bridges that connect cultures through the universal language of food.

THE REGIONAL DIVERSITY OF ITALIAN CUISINE

Italian cuisine is renowned worldwide for its rich and diverse flavors, and one of its most fascinating aspects is the remarkable regional diversity that defines its culinary landscape. Italy, with its varied geography, climate, and historical influences, boasts a mosaic of regional cuisines, each with its own unique ingredients, techniques, and traditions. Exploring the regional diversity of Italian cuisine is like embarking on a culinary journey across the country, offering a taste of Italy's history, culture, and geography in every dish.

THE NORTH: ALPINE INFLUENCES AND CREAMY DELIGHTS

In Northern Italy, the cuisine is shaped by the influence of the Alps and proximity to neighboring countries. The northern regions are known for their creamy risottos, hearty polenta, and abundant use of butter and cheese. For instance:

- **Lombardy:** Famous for its rich risottos, Milan, the regional capital, is known for its saffron-infused Risotto alla Milanese. Lombardy is also home to the beloved creamy cheese, Gorgonzola.

- **Piedmont:** Renowned for its truffles, Piedmont offers dishes like Tagliatelle al Tartufo, a pasta dish adorned with shaved truffles. It's also the birthplace of the slow food movement, emphasizing local, sustainable ingredients.

- **Veneto:** Known for its seafood-rich cuisine, Veneto delights with dishes like Risotto al Nero di Seppia (risotto with squid ink) and the iconic Venetian appetizer, Cicchetti.

CENTRAL ITALY: THE HEARTLAND OF TRADITION

Central Italy is often considered the heartland of Italian cuisine, boasting a balance of fresh coastal ingredients and hearty, rustic dishes. This region is famous for its pasta, olive oil, and wines. Some highlights include:

- **Tuscany:** Known for its rustic and simple yet flavorful dishes, Tuscany offers classics like Ribollita (a hearty soup), Pappa al Pomodoro (tomato and bread soup), and the iconic Florentine steak, Bistecca alla Fiorentina.

- **Lazio:** Home to the capital, Rome, Lazio

showcases dishes like Cacio e Pepe (cheese and pepper pasta) and Carbonara. The artichoke, prepared in various ways, is another regional specialty.

- **Umbria:** Known as the "Green Heart of Italy," Umbria offers a taste of the countryside with dishes like Porchetta (roast pork) and Umbricelli pasta, often served with black truffles.

SOUTHERN ITALY: SUN-KISSED FLAVORS AND MEDITERRANEAN DELIGHTS

Southern Italy, with its warm Mediterranean climate, is celebrated for its vibrant, sun-kissed flavors and abundant use of tomatoes, olive oil, and fresh seafood. Some notable southern regions include:

- **Campania:** Home to Naples and the birthplace of pizza, Campania is famous for its Margherita and Marinara pizza styles. It's also known for dishes like Spaghetti alle Vongole (spaghetti with clams) and Eggplant Parmesan.

- **Sicily:** with a rich history of influences from Arabic, Greek, and Spanish cultures, Sicilian cuisine features dishes like Arancini (rice balls), Caponata (a sweet and sour eggplant dish), and Cannoli, a famous dessert.

- **Puglia:** Known for its simple yet flavorful cuisine, Puglia offers dishes like Orecchiette with Broccoli Rabe and Pecorino cheese, and Burrata cheese, a creamy delicacy.

THE ISLANDS: SARDINIA AND SICILY

Sardinia and Sicily, the two major Italian islands, have unique cuisines deeply rooted in their distinct histories and landscapes. Sardinian cuisine is characterized by hearty, rustic dishes, while Sicilian cuisine is a fusion of Mediterranean flavors and diverse influences.

- **Sardinia:** Known for its pecorino cheese, Sardinia offers dishes like Malloreddus, a type of pasta, and Porceddu, roasted suckling pig.

- **Sicily:** Sicilian cuisine boasts a diverse range of dishes, including Arancini, Pasta alla Norma, and Granita, a refreshing dessert made with ice and fruit flavors.

THE ISLANDS: SICILY AND SARDINIA

Sardinia and Sicily, the two major Italian islands, have unique cuisines deeply rooted in their distinct histories and landscapes. Sardinian cuisine is characterized by hearty, rustic dishes, while Sicilian cuisine is a fusion of Mediterranean flavors and diverse influences.

- **Sardinia:** Known for its pecorino cheese, Sardinia offers dishes like Malloreddus, a type of pasta, and Porceddu, roasted suckling pig.

- **Sicily:** Sicilian cuisine boasts a diverse range of dishes, including Arancini, Pasta alla Norma, and Granita, a refreshing dessert made with ice and fruit flavors.

CHAPTER 2: THE ITALIAN KITCHEN ESSENTIALS

THE STAPLE INGREDIENTS OF ITALIAN COOKING

Italian cuisine is celebrated for its rich and diverse flavors, and at the heart of this culinary tradition are the staple ingredients that have been cherished for centuries. These ingredients serve as the building blocks of Italian cooking, each playing a crucial role in creating the vibrant and harmonious flavors that define Italian dishes. From the golden olive oil to the pungent garlic, from the earthy pasta to the aromatic herbs, these staples are the essence of Italian cuisine.

OLIVE OIL: LIQUID GOLD OF THE MEDITERRANEAN

Olive oil is often referred to as the "liquid gold" of Italian cuisine, and with good reason. It is a fundamental element in Italian cooking, used both as a cooking medium and a flavor enhancer. Italy is one of the world's top producers of olive oil, and each region boasts its own unique varieties and flavors.

Extra-virgin olive oil, prized for its rich, fruity taste and low acidity, is the gold standard in Italian kitchens. It is used for drizzling over salads, finishing dishes, and sautéing vegetables and meats. The choice of olive oil can greatly influence the flavor of a dish, and Italians take great care in selecting the right one to complement their ingredients.

The olive tree is deeply rooted in Italian culture, and olive oil production is a time-honored tradition. The quality of the oil is a point of pride for Italian producers, and it is not uncommon for families to have their own olive trees and produce their oil, often using traditional methods that have been passed down through generations.

GARLIC AND ONIONS: THE AROMATIC BACKBONE

Garlic and onions are the aromatic backbone of Italian cuisine. They form the foundation of many Italian dishes, lending depth and complexity to sauces, soups, and stews. The pungent bite of garlic, when sautéed gently in olive oil, releases its aroma, signaling the start of a delicious meal. Onions, with their sweetness and earthiness, add a harmonious note to a wide range of Italian recipes.

The use of garlic and onions is artfully balanced in Italian cooking. They are often the first ingredients to hit the pan, infusing the cooking oil with their flavors before other ingredients are added. The precise timing of their introduction can greatly influence the final taste of a dish, whether it's a simple tomato sauce, a savory risotto, or a slow-cooked ragù.

HERBS AND SPICES: A DELICATE BALANCE

Herbs and spices play a vital role in Italian cuisine, but their use is marked by a sense of restraint. Italians value the natural flavors of ingredients and use herbs and spices judiciously to enhance, rather than overpower, the dishes they prepare.

Basil is one of the most iconic herbs in Italian cooking, most famously used in pesto. Its sweet, aromatic flavor is a perfect match for tomatoes and fresh mozzarella in the classic Caprese salad. Oregano, with its earthy and slightly peppery notes, is a common addition to pizza and tomato sauces. Rosemary and thyme lend a fragrant touch to roasted meats and vegetables, while sage is often used with butter to create flavorful sauces for pasta and gnocchi.

The use of spices is more sparing in Italian cuisine compared to some other culinary traditions. However, certain dishes call for specific spices, such as saffron in the famous risotto alla Milanese or red pepper flakes to add heat to pasta dishes. The balance of herbs and spices is a delicate art, ensuring that they enhance the natural flavors of the ingredients without overpowering them.

TOMATOES: THE SOUL OF ITALIAN SAUCES

Tomatoes are synonymous with Italian cuisine and serve as the soul of many Italian sauces.

From the vibrant red of fresh tomatoes to the concentrated richness of tomato paste, this ingredient is a cornerstone of countless Italian recipes. Tomatoes bring a sweet-tartness and a burst of color to dishes, elevating them to new heights of flavor.

The classic Italian tomato sauce, marinara, is a simple yet powerful representation of the essence of Italian cooking. Made with just tomatoes, olive oil, garlic, and basil, marinara embodies the Italian philosophy of simplicity and purity of flavor. Other tomato-based sauces, such as pomodoro, arrabbiata, and puttanesca, showcase the versatility of this staple ingredient.

Tomatoes are used in a wide range of dishes, from pasta and pizza to soups and stews. In the summer months, Italians celebrate the bounty of ripe tomatoes with dishes like insalata caprese, a salad of tomatoes, fresh mozzarella, basil, and olive oil—a testament to the beauty of using the freshest ingredients available.

PASTA: A CULINARY CANVAS

Pasta is perhaps Italy's most famous culinary export, and it serves as a versatile and beloved staple in Italian cuisine. with an astonishing array of shapes and sizes, pasta is the canvas upon which Italian flavors are painted.

Fresh pasta, made by hand or with the help of a pasta machine, has a tender, melt-in-your-mouth quality that is hard to match. It can be used to create delicate dishes like ravioli and tagliatelle, each with its unique filling or sauce. Dried pasta, readily available in every Italian pantry, offers convenience without sacrificing flavor or texture. It comes in various shapes, from the elegant strands of spaghetti to the robust tubes of rigatoni, each suited to specific sauces and preparations.

The choice of pasta is crucial in Italian cooking, as different shapes hold sauces in distinctive ways. For example, the ridges of penne are perfect for capturing chunky tomato sauces, while the twists of fusilli pair well with creamy sauces that cling to every curve.

CHEESE: FROM PARMESAN TO MOZZARELLA

Cheese is another staple ingredient that plays a significant role in Italian cuisine. Italy is renowned for its cheese production, and there is a wide variety of cheeses used in both cooking and as table cheeses.

Parmigiano-Reggiano, often referred to as the "King of Cheeses," is a hard, aged cheese with a nutty and salty flavor. It is grated generously over pasta dishes and risottos, adding depth and richness to the flavors. Pecorino Romano, made from sheep's milk, offers a sharp and tangy contrast in dishes like cacio e pepe

Mozzarella, with its creamy texture and mild flavor, is the star of the classic Caprese salad and is a staple on pizza. Ricotta, a soft, fresh cheese, is used in both savory and sweet dishes, from lasagna to cannoli. Gorgonzola, a blue cheese, adds a bold and distinctive flavor to salads and pasta sauces.

PROSCIUTTO AND CURED MEATS

Cured meats, or salumi, are an integral part of Italian cuisine and are often enjoyed as antipasti (appetizers) or incorporated into dishes. Prosciutto di Parma, a renowned dry-cured ham, is prized for its delicate, sweet-savory flavor and silky texture. It is often served thinly sliced and draped over fresh melon or wrapped around grissini (breadsticks).

Other popular cured meats include pancetta, a type of Italian bacon that is used to add depth and richness to sauces and soups, and salami, which comes in various regional varieties, each with its own distinct flavor profile. Cured meats are appreciated for their ability to impart complexity and umami to a wide range of dishes.

THE HOLY TRINITY OF ITALIAN COOKING: TOMATOES, GARLIC, AND BASIL

The combination of tomatoes, garlic, and basil is often referred to as the "holy trinity" of Italian cooking. This trio of ingredients forms the basis for many beloved Italian dishes, and their harmonious interplay is emblematic of the Italian approach to flavor.

Tomatoes provide a sweet-tart base, garlic adds depth and aroma, and basil infuses dishes with a fresh, herbaceous note. Together, they create a symphony of flavors that is both comforting and irresistible. Whether it's a classic Margherita pizza with its simple but sublime toppings or a tomato and garlic-infused pasta sauce, this combination embodies the essence of Italian cuisine.

MUST-HAVE TOOLS AND UTENSILS

PASTA MACHINE

A pasta machine is an essential tool for any Italian kitchen. It allows you to roll out pasta dough to the perfect thickness and cut it into various shapes, from fettuccine to lasagna sheets. Freshly made pasta, whether it's tagliatelle, pappardelle, or ravioli, has a delicate texture and flavor that is hard to match with store-bought alternatives. Invest in a good-quality pasta machine to enjoy the true essence of Italian pasta.

WOODEN PASTA DRYING RACK

After making fresh pasta, you'll need a wooden pasta drying rack to hang and dry the pasta. This traditional tool ensures that the pasta dries evenly and prevents it from sticking together. Wooden racks are preferred because they absorb excess moisture, which can affect the pasta's texture. Whether you're making spaghetti, linguine, or orecchiette, a pasta drying rack is indispensable.

PIZZA STONE

For those who love making pizza at home, a pizza stone is a game-changer. It helps achieve the crispy, charred crust that is characteristic of authentic Italian pizza. The stone absorbs and distributes heat evenly, resulting in a perfectly cooked pizza with a wonderful, slightly smoky flavor. A pizza peel, a flat wooden paddle, is also useful for transferring the pizza to and from the oven.

MORTAR AND PESTLE

Italian cuisine relies heavily on the use of fresh herbs and spices, and a mortar and pestle are invaluable tools for crushing and grinding ingredients. Whether you're making pesto, grinding spices for a marinade, or mashing garlic for aioli, a mortar and pestle allows you to release the full flavors of your ingredients while maintaining their essential oils and aromas.

CHEESE GRATER

Freshly grated cheese is a common garnish for many Italian dishes, and having a good cheese grater is essential. A box grater with different sized grating surfaces is versatile and suitable for grating Parmesan, Pecorino Romano, or other hard cheeses. Freshly grated cheese adds a creamy and flavorful touch to pasta, risotto, salads, and more.

ESPRESSO MACHINE

Coffee is an integral part of Italian culture, and an espresso machine is a must-have for those who appreciate a perfect shot of espresso or a frothy cappuccino. Italians take their coffee seriously, and investing in a high-quality espresso machine will allow you to enjoy café-quality coffee in the comfort of your home. Remember to use freshly ground coffee beans for the best results.

PASTA POT WITH STRAINER INSERT

Cooking pasta to perfection requires a pasta pot with a strainer insert. This specialized pot allows you to easily drain the pasta without having to use a separate colander, which can be cumbersome. The strainer insert lifts out the cooked pasta, leaving the hot pasta water in the pot for making sauces or reheating the pasta before serving.

WOODEN SPATULAS AND SPOONS

Wooden utensils are a staple in Italian kitchens, as they are gentle on cookware and perfect for stirring, sautéing, and serving delicate dishes. Wooden spatulas and spoons are ideal for making risotto, polenta, or any dish that requires constant stirring without damaging the cookware's surface or affecting the flavors.

MEAT TENDERIZER

When preparing dishes like osso buco or scaloppine, a meat tenderizer is essential for pounding meat to the desired thickness and tenderness. It helps break down muscle fibers, making the meat more tender and easier to cook evenly. A dual-sided meat tenderizer with a flat side for flattening and a textured side for tenderizing is versatile for various recipes.

CITRUS ZESTER/GRATER

Italian cuisine often incorporates the zest of lemons, oranges, or other citrus fruits to add brightness and flavor to dishes. A citrus zester or grater allows you to remove the fragrant outer zest without the bitter pith. This tool is essential for making lemon zest for pasta dishes, desserts like tiramisu, or flavoring sauces and vinaigrettes.

POTATO RICER

A potato ricer, also known as a passatutto, is indispensable for making perfectly smooth and fluffy mashed potatoes. It works by pressing boiled potatoes through small holes, resulting in a silky texture without overworking the potatoes and making them gluey. Besides potatoes, it can also be used for making gnocchi and other purees.

BAKING STONE OR STEEL

In addition to pizza, Italian cuisine includes a variety of bread and baked goods. A baking stone or steel helps achieve the ideal oven spring and crispy crust for bread, focaccia, and other baked treats. These tools also distribute heat evenly, ensuring that your baked goods cook uniformly and have the desired texture.

KITCHEN SCALE

Precision is key in Italian baking, and a kitchen scale is crucial for accurately measuring ingredients. Whether you're making fresh pasta, bread, or pastries, a scale allows you to follow recipes with precision and achieve consistent results every time. Many Italian recipes use weight measurements, so a scale is especially helpful.

MICROPLANE GRATER

A microplane grater is a versatile tool for finely grating ingredients such as garlic, ginger, nutmeg, or hard cheeses like Parmesan. Its fine blades create a powdery texture that evenly distributes flavor throughout dishes. This tool is essential for recipes where achieving a fine texture is important.

COLANDER AND SALAD SPINNER

A colander is essential for rinsing and draining pasta, vegetables, and greens. It's also handy for washing and draining canned beans, a staple ingredient in many Italian recipes. A salad spinner, on the other hand, helps remove excess water from washed greens, ensuring that salads stay crisp and sauces adhere properly.

WHISK AND MIXING BOWLS

Whisks come in various shapes and sizes and are essential for blending ingredients, whipping cream, and emulsifying dressings and sauces. A good set of mixing bowls in various sizes is also crucial for preparing and storing ingredients. Stainless steel or glass mixing bowls are preferred for their durability and ease of cleaning.

FINE-MESH SIEVE

A fine-mesh sieve is used for straining liquids, sifting flour, and removing impurities from sauces and soups. It ensures a smooth texture and removes any lumps or solid particles, resulting in silky sauces and velvety custards, which are often used in Italian desserts like panna cotta and zabaglione.

PASTRY BRUSH

A pastry brush, often made of natural bristles or silicone, is used for brushing olive oil, egg wash, or butter onto dough or baked goods. It's essential for achieving a glossy finish on bread, pastries, and even pizza crusts. A pastry brush also helps evenly distribute flavors, such as brushing garlic-infused oil onto bruschetta.

MANDOLINE SLICER

A mandoline slicer is a handy tool for achieving precise and uniform cuts of vegetables, such as thinly sliced zucchini for a gratin or paper-thin rounds of potatoes for a potato dish. It saves time and ensures even cooking, making it a valuable addition to the Italian kitchen.

KITCHEN THERMOMETER

A kitchen thermometer is essential for accurately measuring the internal temperature of meats, poultry, and fish. It ensures that these protein sources are cooked to the correct degree of doneness, preventing undercooking or overcooking. It's particularly useful when preparing dishes like osso buco or roast chicken.

CHAPTER 3: SIDES, SAUCES AND SPICES

SIMPLE ROASTED MUSHROOMS

Prep time: **10 minutes** | Cook time: **20 minutes** | Serves **4**

- 6 portobello mushroom caps
- 1 tsp extra-virgin olive oil
- 2 tsp balsamic vinegar
- Salt and garlic powder to taste
- ¼ cup fresh thyme, chopped
- ¼ cup fresh oregano, chopped

1. Mix all ingredients, except mushrooms, in a large bowl.
2. Add in the mushroom caps, cover with a lid, and refrigerate for at least 2 hours at room temperature.
3. Preheat oven to 400 F.
4. Arrange the mushrooms on a parchment-lined baking sheet.
5. Roast them for 15–20 minutes until cooked.
6. To serve, slice the caps into small wedges.

POTATOES AND PEPPERS

Prep time: **10 minutes** | Cook time: **20 minutes** | Serves **4–6**

- 6 potatoes, cut into ½-inch-thick slices
- 1 cup olive oil, plus more if needed
- Salt, to taste
- 3 yellow bell peppers, sliced
- 3 red bell peppers, sliced

1. Place the potato slices in a bowl of warm water and soak for 20–30 minutes prior to cooking.
2. In a medium-sized saucepan, heat the olive oil over high heat, add the potatoes, and sauté until they begin to brown. Add a pinch of salt and the bell peppers, and continue to cook for 15–20 minutes, until the potatoes are lightly browned and the peppers are soft, stirring often to keep the mixture from sticking to the pan and adding more oil, if necessary. Remove pan from the heat and transfer the potatoes and peppers to a serving bowl. Top with another pinch of salt and serve.

CHEESE & BELL PEPPER STUFFED TOMATOES

Prep time: **10 minutes** | Cook time: **25 minutes** | Serves **2**

- ½ lb mixed bell peppers, chopped
- 1 tbsp olive oil
- 4 tomatoes
- 2 garlic cloves, minced
- ½ cup diced onion
- 1 tbsp chopped oregano
- 1 tbsp chopped basil
- 1 cup shredded mozzarella
- 1 tbsp grated Parmesan cheese
- Salt and black pepper to taste

1. Preheat your oven to 370 F.
2. Cut the tops of the tomatoes and scoop out the pulp.
3. Chop the pulp and set aside.
4. Arrange the tomatoes on a lined parchment paper baking sheet.
5. Warm the olive oil in a pan over medium heat.
6. Add garlic, onion, basil, bell peppers, and oregano, and cook for 5 minutes.
7. Sprinkle with salt and pepper.
8. Remove from the heat and mix in tomato pulp and mozzarella cheese.
9. Divide the mixture between the tomatoes and top with Parmesan cheese.
10. Bake for 20 minutes or until the cheese melts.
11. Serve.

BALSAMIC ROASTED RED PEPPER & OLIVE SPREAD

Prep time: **10 minutes** | Cook time: **none** | Serves **6**

- ¼ tsp dried thyme
- 1 tbsp capers
- ½ cup pitted green olives
- 1 roasted red pepper, chopped
- 1 tsp balsamic vinegar
- 2/3 cup soft bread crumbs
- 2 cloves garlic, minced
- ½ tsp red pepper flakes
- 1/3 cup extra-virgin olive oil

1. Place all ingredients, except olive oil, in a food processor and blend until chunky.
2. with the machine running, slowly pour in the olive oil until well combined.
3. Refrigerate or serve at room temperature.

SWEET POTATO MASH

Prep time: **10 minutes** | Cook time: **30 minutes** | Serves **4**

- ¼ cup mascarpone cheese, softened
- ¼ cup olive oil
- ½ tsp ground nutmeg
- 1 ¼ lb sweet potatoes, cubed
- Salt and black pepper to taste
- 1 tbsp fresh chives, chopped

1. Place the sweet potatoes in a pot over high heat and cover with water.
2. Bring to a boil, then lower the heat and simmer covered for 20 minutes.
3. Drain the potatoes and back to the pot.
4. Stir in mascarpone, olive oil, nutmeg, salt, and pepper.
5. Mash them with a potato masher until smooth.
6. Sprinkle with chives.

BUTTER AND SAGE SAUCE

Prep time: **10 minutes** | Cook time: **3 minutes** | Serves **1**

- 1½ sticks unsalted butter
- 10 fresh sage leaves
- 1 cup very hot water from the cooking pot of your
- pasta of choice
- ¼ teaspoon freshly ground black pepper, or to taste
- 1 cup freshly grated Grana Padano

1. Heat the butter in a large skillet over medium heat until melted and just foaming. Gently lay the sage leaves in the pan, and heat until they crisp up, about a minute.
2. Ladle in 1 cup boiling pasta water; stir the sauce, and simmer for about 2 minutes, to reduce liquid by half. Grind the black pepper directly into the sauce
3. Keep the sauce hot over very low heat; then return sauce to a simmer just before adding the drained pasta. Toss the pasta in the sauce until well coated. Remove from heat and toss in the cheese just before serving.

VARIATION WITH PICKLES AND NO ANCHOVIES

Prep time: **10 minutes** | Cook time: **25 minutes** | Serves **4-6**

- ⅓ cup cornichons or other fine cucumber pickles in vinegar
- 6 green olives in brine
- ½ tablespoon onion chopped very fine
- ⅛ teaspoon garlic chopped very fine
- ¼ cup chopped
- parsley
- 1½ tablespoons freshly squeezed lemon juice
- ½ cup extra virgin olive oil
- salt
- black pepper, ground fresh from the mill

1. Put all the ingredients into the food processor and blend to a uniform consistency, but do not overprocess.
2. Taste and correct for salt and tartness. If you decide to add more vinegar or lemon juice, do so a little at a time, retasting each time to avoid making the sauce too sharp.

WARM RED SAUCE

Prep time: **10 minutes** | Cook time: **25 minutes** | Serves **4**

- 3 meaty red or yellow bell peppers
- 5 medium yellow onions, peeled and sliced thin
- ¼ cup vegetable oil
- a tiny pinch chopped hot chili pepper
- 2 cups canned imported Italian plum tomatoes, with their juice, or 3 cups cut-up fresh tomatoes, if very ripe
- salt

1. Split the peppers lengthwise, and remove the core and seeds. Skin the peppers, using a peeler, and cut them into slices more or less ½ inch wide.
2. Put the onions and oil in a saucepan and turn on the heat to medium. Cook the onions, stirring, until wilted and soft, but not brown.
3. Add the peppers, and continue cooking over medium heat until both peppers and onions are very soft and their bulk has been reduced by half. Add the chili pepper, the tomatoes, and salt and continue cooking, letting the sauce simmer gently, for 25 minutes or so, until the tomatoes and oil separate and the fat floats free. Taste and correct for salt, and serve hot.

PIQUANT GREEN SAUCE

Prep time: **10 minutes** | Cook time: **25 minutes** | Serves **4-6**

- ⅔ cup parsley leaves
- 2½ tablespoons capers
- Optional:
- 6 flat anchovy fillets
- ½ teaspoon garlic chopped very fine
- ½ teaspoon strong mustard
- salt
- ½ teaspoon (depending on taste) red wine vinegar, if the sauce is for meat, or 1 tablespoon (depending on taste) fresh lemon juice, if for fish
- ½ cup extra virgin olive oil

1. Put all the ingredients into the food processor and blend to a uniform consistency, but do not overprocess.
2. Taste and correct for salt and tartness. If you decide to add more vinegar or lemon juice, do so a little at a time, retasting each time to avoid making the sauce too sharp.

MASHED CARROTS

Prep time: **10 minutes** | Cook time: **30 minutes** | Serves **4**

- 8–10 carrots, peeled and chopped
- 2 teaspoons brown sugar
- ¼ cup salted butter
- 1 cup heavy cream
- ¼ cup freshly grated Parmesan cheese
- Salt, to taste

1. In a large saucepan, place the carrots and cover with water. Add the brown sugar, bring to a boil over medium-high heat, and cook for 15–20 minutes, until carrots are soft. Remove from heat.
2. Drain carrots, return to the saucepan and mash with a masher. Add the butter and some of the heavy cream, place the pan over low heat, and warm the mashed carrots, stirring occasionally, for 10 minutes. Gradually add the remaining cream until the mixture is smooth. Add the cheese and a pinch of salt, and stir to combine thoroughly. Remove from the heat and serve warm.

CLASSIC PESTO

Prep time: **10 minutes** | Cook time: **none** | Serves **4**

- 4 cups loosely packed fresh basil leaves, gently washed and dried
- ¼ teaspoon kosher salt
- 2 garlic cloves
- 3 tablespoons pine nuts, toasted
- 2 tablespoons freshly grated Pecorino Romano
- 2 tablespoons freshly grated Grana Padano
- 3 to 4 tablespoons extra-virgin olive oil

1. To make the pesto in a mortar: Place a few basil leaves in the bottom of a mortar, and sprinkle the salt over them. Crush the leaves coarsely with the pestle, add a few more leaves, and continue crushing, adding new leaves each time those in the mortar are crushed, until all the leaves are coarsely ground. Toss in the garlic, and pound until the mixture forms a smooth paste. Add the pine nuts, and grind them to a paste. Stir in the cheese, then enough of the olive oil to give the pesto a creamy consistency.
2. To make the pesto in a food processor: Combine the basil, salt, and garlic in the work bowl, add 2 tablespoons of the oil, and blend at low speed, stopping frequently to press the basil down around the blades, until the basil forms a coarse paste. Toss in the pine nuts, and pour in the remaining 2 tablespoons olive oil. Blend until the pine nuts are finely ground. Stir in the grated cheeses.
3. Pesto is at its best when used immediately after it is made, though it can be refrigerated for up to a few weeks if it's spooned into a container, topped with olive oil, and sealed tightly to minimize oxidation. If you find yourself with an abundance of basil in the summer, make some pesto and store it in jars or containers, in portions, in the freezer, where it will last for several months.
4. To serve: Toss the pesto with the cooked drained pasta, adding a few spoons of the pasta-cooking water. Pesto should not be heated or cooked, because it loses its fragrance.

RAW SUMMER TOMATO SAUCE FOR PASTA

Prep time: **10 minutes** | Cook time: **2 hours** | Serves **3 to**

- 2 pounds ripe summer tomatoes
- 2 to 3 garlic cloves
- ½ teaspoon kosher salt
- 6 large basil leaves
- ¼ teaspoon crushed red pepper flakes, or to taste
- ½ cup extra-virgin olive oil
- 1 cup or more freshly grated Grana Padano or cubed fresh mozzarella (optional)

1. Rinse the tomatoes, drain, and wipe dry. Cut out the core and any other tough parts. Working over a big mixing bowl to catch all the juices, cut the tomatoes—cherry tomatoes in half, regular tomatoes into 1-inch chunks—and drop them in the bowl.
2. Smash the garlic cloves with a chef's knife, peel, and chop into a fine paste (easier if you add some of the salt as you chop; mash the garlic bits and salt with the flat side of the knife, too). Scatter the garlic paste and the rest of the salt (½ teaspoon in all) over the tomatoes, and stir gently. Pile up the basil leaves and cut into thin strips. Scatter these over the tomatoes, then sprinkle in the crushed red pepper. Pour in the oil; stir and fold to coat the tomatoes and distribute the seasonings.
3. Cover the bowl with plastic wrap, and let the sauce marinate at room temperature for 1 to 2 hours. Toss the marinated sauce with freshly cooked and drained pasta. Serve as is, or toss in 1 cup grated Grana Padano, or for extra richness, add 1 cup or more cubed fresh mozzarella.

BASIL, PARSLEY, AND WALNUT PESTO

Prep time: **10 minutes** | Cook time: **none** | Serves **4**

- 1½ cups loosely packed fresh basil leaves
- 1 cup loosely packed fresh Italian parsley leaves
- 4 garlic cloves
- 2 cups walnut halves or pieces, toasted
- 1 teaspoon kosher
- salt
- ½ cup extra-virgin olive oil
- 1 cup freshly grated Pecorino Romano (or half pecorino and half Grana Padano, for a milder flavor), plus more for passing

1. Combine the basil, parsley, garlic, walnuts, and salt in the work bowl of a food processor. Pulse several times, to chop everything together coarsely; then, with the machine running, pour in the ½ cup olive oil in a slow, steady stream. Stop and scrape down the sides of the work bowl, and process to a uniformly fine bright green pesto.
2. To store and use the pesto later: Scrape it from the food processor into a small jar or container. Smooth the top surface, and cover it with a thin layer of olive oil or a piece of plastic wrap to prevent discoloration. Refrigerate up to a week, or freeze for several months; warm to room temperature before using. Combine with the cheese only when you sauce the pasta.
3. To serve: Toss the hot drained pasta with the pesto, adding a few spoons of pasta-cooking water. Do not heat the pesto—it loses its fragrance.

ZUCCHINI AND POTATO PARMESAN

Prep time: **10 minutes** | Cook time: **55 minutes** | Serves **4–6**

- 6 russet potatoes, peeled and cut into ½-inch slices
- Olive oil
- Salt
- 6 fresh zucchini, cut into ¼-inch slices
- 3 eggs
- 1½ cups panna di cucina or heavy cream
- Pinch of black pepper
- ¼ cup chopped fresh basil
- ¼ cup chopped fresh parsley
- 2 cups grated Mozzarella cheese
- 1 cup freshly grated Parmesan cheese
- ½ cup breadcrumbs

1. Place the potato slices in a large bowl of hot water and allow to soak for 2 hours.
2. Preheat the oven to 350°F and grease two baking sheets with olive oil.
3. Arrange potatoes on the prepared baking sheets. Drizzle more olive oil over the potatoes and generously sprinkle with salt. Bake for 15–20 minutes. Repeat this baking process with the zucchini, but omit the salt and bake for only 5 minutes. Whisk the eggs, panna, and black pepper in a bowl and set aside.
4. In a large casserole dish (see Note), arrange your ingredients in layers: Place a layer of potatoes on the bottom of the dish and brush with some egg mixture. Add a layer of zucchini and sprinkle with the herbs. Add a layer of the Mozzarella cheese and then add a layer of the Parmesan cheese. Repeat this layering process until the whole casserole dish is full. Pour the remaining egg mixture over the top, and, finally, add a layer of breadcrumbs. Bake, covered with a lid or foil, for 30 minutes.

PEPPERY SAUCE FOR BOILED MEATS

Prep time: **10 minutes** | Cook time: **15 minutes** | Makes about 1 cup

- 1 cup beef marrow chopped very fine
- 1½ tablespoons butter
- 3 tablespoons fine, dry, unflavored bread crumbs
- 2 or more cups Basic Homemade Meat Broth, prepared as directed on
- salt
- black pepper, ground fresh from the mill

1. Put the marrow and butter into a small saucepan. If you have one, a flameproof earthenware would be ideal for this kind of slow cooking, and enameled cast iron would be a suitable alternative. Turn on the heat to medium, and stir frequently, mashing the marrow with a wooden spoon.
2. When the marrow and butter have melted and begin to foam, put in the bread crumbs. Cook the crumbs for a minute or two, turning them in the fat.
3. Add ⅓ cup broth. Cook over slow heat, stirring with the wooden spoon while the broth evaporates and the crumbs thicken. Add 2 or 3 pinches of salt and a very liberal quantity of ground pepper.
4. Continue to add broth, a little at a time, letting it evaporate before adding more. Stir frequently, and keep the heat low. The final consistency should be creamy and thick, without any lumps. Taste and correct for salt and pepper. If the sauce is too dense for your taste, thin it by cooking it briefly with more broth. Serve hot over sliced boiled meat, or in a sauceboat on the side.

MEAT SAUCE BOLOGNESE

Prep time: **10 minutes** | Cook time: **3 hours 30 minutes** | Serves **6**

- 3 tablespoons extra-virgin olive oil
- 1 medium yellow onion, minced (about 1 cup)
- 1 medium carrot, peeled and finely shredded (about ½ cup)
- ½ cup minced celery, with leaves
- 1 pound ground beef
- 1 pound ground pork
- ½ cup dry red wine
- 1 tablespoon tomato paste
- 3 cups canned Italian plum tomatoes, preferably San Marzano, crushed by hand or passed through a food mill
- 3 fresh bay leaves
- 2 teaspoons kosher salt
- Freshly ground black pepper to taste

1. Bring 4 cups water to a simmer in a small saucepan, and keep hot. Heat the olive oil in a large Dutch oven over medium heat. When the oil is hot, add the onion, carrot, and celery, and cook, stirring, until the onion is translucent, about 7 minutes.
2. Crumble in the ground beef and pork, and continue cooking, stirring to break up the meat, until all the liquid the meat has given off has evaporated and the meat is lightly browned, about 10 minutes.
3. Pour in the wine, and cook, scraping the bottom of the pan, until the wine is evaporated, 3 to 4 minutes. Add in the tomato paste into a bare spot in the pan and cook a few minutes, then pour in the tomatoes, toss in the bay leaves, and season with the salt and some pepper. Bring to a boil, then lower the heat so the sauce is at a lively simmer. Cook, stirring occasionally, until the sauce is dense but juicy and a rich dark red color. This will take about 2 to 3 hours—the longer you cook it, the better it will become. While the sauce is cooking, add hot water as necessary to keep the meats and vegetables covered. (Most likely, a noticeable layer of oil will float to the top toward the end of cooking. When you are done, the oil can be removed with a spoon or reincorporated in the sauce, which is what is traditionally done.)

A PEPPERY SAUCE FOR ROAST BIRDS

Prep time: **10 minutes** | Cook time: **35 minutes** | Serves **6 or more**

- ¼ pound mild pork sausage
- ¼ pound chicken livers
- 1 ounce cucumber pickles in vinegar, preferably cornichons
- ⅓ cup extra virgin olive oil, or less if the sausage is very fatty
- 1 tablespoon onion chopped very fine
- salt
- black pepper, ground fresh from the mill
- 1½ teaspoons grated lemon peel, carefully avoiding the white pith beneath it
- ⅔ cup dry white wine

1. Skin the sausage. Put the sausage meat, chicken livers, and pickles into a food processor and chop to a thick, creamy consistency.
2. Put the olive oil and onion in a small saucepan, turn on the heat to medium, and cook the onion until it becomes colored a pale gold. Add the chopped sausage mixture, stirring thoroughly to coat it well.
3. Add salt and liberal grindings of pepper. Stir well. Add the grated lemon peel, and stir thoroughly once again.
4. Add the wine, stir once or twice, then adjust heat to cook the sauce at a very gentle, steady simmer, and cover the pan. Cook for 1 hour, stirring occasionally. If you find the sauce becoming too dense or dry, add 1 or 2 tablespoons of water.
5. Serve hot over cut-up pieces or carved breast slices of roast birds.

CHAPTER 4: SALADS AND SOUPS

ASPARAGUS SALAD

Prep time: **10 minutes** | Cook time: **10 minutes** | Serves **4**

- 4 tbsp olive oil
- 1 lb asparagus
- 1 garlic clove, minced
- Salt and black pepper to taste
- 1 tbsp balsamic vinegar
- 1 tbsp lemon zest

1. In a greased skillet, roast the asparagus over medium heat for 5-6 minutes, turning once.
2. Season to taste.
3. Toss with garlic, olive oil, lemon zest, and vinegar.
4. Serve.

PORK MEATBALL SOUP

Prep time: **10 minutes** | Cook time: **35 minutes** | Serves **4**

- 2 tbsp olive oil
- ½ cup white rice
- ½ lb ground pork
- Salt and black pepper to taste
- 2 garlic cloves, minced
- 1 onion, chopped
- ½ tsp dried thyme
- 4 cups beef stock
- ½ tsp saffron powder
- 14 oz canned tomatoes, diced
- 1 tbsp parsley, chopped

1. In a large bowl, mix ground pork, rice, salt, and pepper with your hands.
2. Shape the mixture into ½-inch balls; set aside.
3. Warm the olive oil in a pot over medium heat and cook the onion and garlic for 5 minutes.
4. Pour in beef stock, thyme, saffron powder, and tomatoes and bring to a boil.
5. Add in the pork balls and cook for 20 minutes.
6. Adjust the seasoning with salt and pepper.
7. Serve sprinkled with parsley.

POTATO SOUP WITH SPLIT GREEN PEAS

Prep time: **10 minutes** | Cook time: **35 minutes** | Serves **6**

- 2 medium boiling potatoes
- ½ pound split dried green peas
- 5 cups Basic Homemade Meat Broth, prepared as directed on , or 1 cup canned beef broth diluted with 4 cups water or 1 bouillon cube dissolved in 5 cups water
- 3 tablespoons butter
- 3 tablespoons vegetable oil
- 2 tablespoons chopped onion
- 3 tablespoons freshly grated parmigiano-reggiano cheese, plus additional cheese at the table
- salt
- crostini, fried bread squares, made as directed on

1. Peel the potatoes and cut them up into small pieces. Rinse in cold water and drain.
2. Rinse the split peas in cold water and drain.
3. Put the potatoes and peas in a soup pot together with 3 cups of broth, cover, turn on the heat to medium, and cook at a gentle boil until both the potatoes and the peas are tender. Turn off the heat.
4. Purée the potatoes and peas with their liquid through a food mill back into the pot.
5. Put the butter and vegetable oil in a small skillet, add the chopped onion, turn on the heat to medium high. Cook the onion, stirring it, until it becomes colored a rich gold.
6. Pour the entire contents of the skillet into the pot with the potatoes and peas, add the remaining 2 cups of broth, cover, and turn on the heat to medium, adjusting it so that the soup bubbles at a steady, but slow boil. Cook, stirring from time to time, until any floating butter and oil has become evenly distributed into the broth.
7. Before turning off the heat, swirl in the grated Parmesan, then taste and correct for salt. Ladle into individual plates or bowls and serve with crostini on the side and additional grated Parmesan for the table.

ESCAROLE AND WHITE BEAN SOUP

Prep time: **10 minutes** | Cook time: **2 hours 1 minutes** | Serves **6**

- 1½ cups dried cannellini, Great Northern, baby lima, or other small white beans
- 2 fresh bay leaves
- ½ cup extra-virgin olive oil
- Kosher salt to taste
- 6 cups (approximately 1 head) coarsely shredded escarole leaves (preferably the tough outer leaves), washed and drained
- 8 garlic cloves, cut in half
- 4 to 6 whole dried peperoncini (hot red peppers)
- Garlic bread or plain grilled country bread, for serving

1. The day before you want to make the soup, put the beans in a 2-to-3-quart container and pour in enough cold water to cover them by at least 4 inches. Let soak in a cool place at least 8 hours, or up to 24 hours.
2. Drain the beans thoroughly, and transfer to a large stockpot. Pour in 2 quarts of water, toss in the bay leaves, and bring to a boil. Adjust the heat to simmering, pour in half of the olive oil, and cook until the beans are tender and only an inch of liquid remains, 1 to 1½ hours.
3. Season the beans to taste with salt, then stir in the escarole and cook, stirring occasionally, until the escarole is quite tender, about 15 minutes. Remove bay leaves.
4. Heat the remaining olive oil in a small skillet over medium heat. Add the garlic and peppers and cook, shaking the pan, until the peppers change color, about 1 minute or less. Remove from the heat, and carefully— it will sputter quite a bit—pour one ladleful of soup into the skillet. Swirl the pan to blend the two, and then stir the panful of seasoned soup back into the large pot. Give it a boil, check the seasoning, and let the soup rest off the heat, covered, 10 to 15 minutes. Serve with garlic bread if you like, or grilled country bread.

CITRUSY SHRIMP & CALAMARI SALAD

Prep time: **10 minutes** | Cook time: **6 minutes** | Serves **4–6**

- Juice of 2 lemons (about ¼ cup/2 fl oz/60 ml)
- 2 tablespoons red wine vinegar
- 1 tablespoon Dijon mustard
- 1 clove garlic, crushed in a garlic press
- Fine sea salt and freshly ground black pepper
- 1 lb (500 g) cleaned calamari bodies and tentacles
- 1 lb (500 g) large shrimp, peeled and deveined
- ¼ cup (1 oz/30 g) thinly sliced red onion
- 1 small fresh hot chile, thinly sliced crosswise, or a generous pinch of red pepper flakes
- 2 tablespoons coarsely chopped fresh flat-leaf parsley
- 2 fresh bay leaves, or 4 dried bay leaves
- 3 long strips lemon zest
- Crusty bread for serving

1. In a small bowl, whisk together the lemon juice, vinegar, mustard, garlic, 1 teaspoon salt, and a generous grinding of pepper. Set aside.
2. Bring a large pot of water to a boil over high heat. Cut the calamari bodies into rings ¾ inch (2 cm) thick. Add the calamari rings and tentacles to the boiling water and cook for 2 minutes. Add the shrimp and cook until all the seafood is opaque throughout but still tender, about 4 minutes longer. Drain well and transfer to a bowl.
3. Pour the dressing over the seafood. It will seem like a lot, but the ample amount is necessary for marinating. Add the onion, chile, and parsley and stir to mix well. Tuck in the bay leaves and lemon zest, cover, and refrigerate until well chilled, at least 2 hours. Stir occasionally so that all the pieces marinate thoroughly.
4. Discard the lemon zest and the bay leaves. Divide the salad among small plates and serve with the bread on the side for sopping up the juices.

ROASTED EGGPLANT AND TOMATO SALAD

Prep time: **10 minutes** | Cook time: **30 minutes** | Serves **6**

- 2 medium eggplants (about 1¼ pounds)
- 4 tablespoons extra-virgin olive oil
- ½ teaspoon kosher salt, plus more to taste
- 3 cups ripe grape or small cherry tomatoes
- ¼ teaspoon freshly ground black pepper
- ¼ cup red wine vinegar
- 12 small fresh basil leaves, or 2 tablespoons shredded large fresh basil leaves
- ⅓ cup shredded fresh mozzarella or ricotta salata

1. Preheat the oven to 450 degrees. Trim the ends of the eggplants and slice crosswise into 1-inch-thick rounds; cut each round into halves or quarters, to make roughly equal pieces no bigger than 2 inches on a side. Put the chunks on a baking sheet lined with parchment, and sprinkle over them 1 tablespoon oil and ¼ teaspoon salt. Toss well.
2. Put the tomatoes on another parchment-lined sheet pan, sprinkle over them 1 tablespoon oil and a pinch of salt, roll them around, and spread them out. Put both sheets in the oven, and roast until both the eggplant and the tomatoes are soft, shriveled, and nicely caramelized on the edges, 30 minutes or more. Turn the eggplant chunks a couple of times while roasting, roll the tomatoes over, and shift the sheets around in the oven for even heating.
3. Let the vegetables cool completely on the sheets, then transfer to a large mixing bowl. Toss gently with the remaining 2 tablespoons olive oil, ¼ teaspoon salt, some ground pepper, the vinegar, and basil. Taste, and adjust the seasonings. Arrange the salad on a serving platter or portion on salad plates, and sprinkle the shredded cheese on top.

MUSHROOM SOUP

Prep time: **10 minutes** | Cook time: **1 hour 20 minutes** | Serves **2½ to 3**

- 1 cup loosely packed dried porcini mushrooms
- ¼ cup extra-virgin olive oil, plus more for drizzling
- 2 large shallots, chopped
- 1 large carrot, peeled, shredded on the coarse holes of a box grater or in a food processor
- 1½ pounds russet potatoes, peeled, shredded on the coarse holes of a box grater or in a food processor
- 2 tablespoons chopped fresh sage
- 1 tablespoon kosher salt
- One 3-inch piece Grana Padano rind, rinsed
- 2 pounds mixed mushrooms, thickly sliced (button, cremini, shiitake, oyster, chanterelle, porcini)
- ½ cup chopped fresh Italian parsley
- Freshly grated Grana Padano, for serving

1. Put porcini in a spouted measuring cup, and add 1 cup very hot water. Let soak until softened, about 10 minutes. Squeeze the porcini dry, reserving the soaking liquid. Chop the porcini and strain the soaking liquid through cheesecloth.
2. To a large Dutch oven over medium heat, add the olive oil. When the oil is hot, add the shallots and sweat until wilted, about 5 minutes. Add the carrot and potatoes, and increase the heat to medium high. Cook until the potatoes begin to stick to the bottom of the pan, about 5 minutes, stirring occasionally. Add 5 quarts cold water, the porcini-soaking liquid, sage, salt, and cheese rind. Bring to a boil, and simmer to blend the flavors, about 20 minutes.
3. Add the sliced mushrooms and chopped soaked dried porcini. Return the soup to a boil. Simmer rapidly until the potatoes have dissolved to thicken the soup and the mushrooms are very tender, about 40 minutes. Stir in the parsley, and remove and discard the cheese rind. Serve the soup with a drizzle of olive oil and a sprinkle of grated cheese.

STRING BEAN SALAD WITH RICOTTA SALATA & LEMON

Prep time: **10 minutes** | Cook time: **5 minutes** | Serves **4**

- ½ lb (250 g) yellow (wax) beans, stem ends removed
- ½ lb (250 g) green beans, stem ends removed
- 1 large ripe tomato, cut into bite-size chunks
- 2–3 tablespoons lemon-infused olive oil or extra-virgin olive oil
- Finely grated zest of ½ lemon
- Fine sea salt and freshly ground black pepper
- 8 fresh basil leaves, preferably 4 green and 4 purple, finely shredded
- 2 tablespoons crumbled ricotta salata cheese

1. Place a steamer basket in a large saucepan and fill the pan with water up to but not touching the bottom of the basket. Bring the water to a boil over high heat. Add the beans to the basket, cover, and steam until just tender-crisp, 4–5 minutes. The green beans should be bright green.

2. Transfer the beans to a large salad bowl. Add the tomato, sprinkle with the olive oil and lemon zest, and toss to mix. Add ¼ teaspoon salt, a small grinding of pepper, the basil ribbons, and the cheese, toss again, and serve.

GRAPEFRUIT, FENNEL & BURRATA SALAD

Prep time: **10 minutes** | Cook time: **none** | Serves **4**

- 1 Ruby grapefruit
- 1 white grapefruit
- 1 small fennel bulb, halved, cored, and cut lengthwise into very thin slices, plus 1 tablespoon chopped fennel fronds
- 1–2 tablespoons honey
- Fine sea salt and freshly ground black pepper
- 2 tablespoons extra-virgin olive oil
- 1 small ball (4 oz/125 g) burrata cheese

1. Set a colander over a bowl. Using a serrated knife, cut off the tops and bottoms of the grapefruits. Then slice from top to bottom to remove the rind and bitter white pith. Holding the grapefruit over the colander, cut the segments of fruit from the membranes, letting the segments fall into the colander. Let drain for about 5 minutes, then transfer the segments to a separate bowl and add the fennel bulb slices.

2. Transfer 2 tablespoons of the grapefruit juice to a small bowl and whisk in 1–2 tablespoons honey, depending on how sweet the juice is. Season with ½ teaspoon salt and a few grindings of pepper. Whisk in the olive oil until the dressing is emulsified.

3. Drizzle the dressing over the grapefruit and fennel and toss gently to combine. Spoon the salad onto a serving plate or shallow bowl.

4. Slice the cheese in half and scoop out the creamy filling with a spoon. Chop the "skin," or exterior, into small pieces. Scatter the filling and chopped pieces over the salad. Sprinkle the fennel fronds on top and season with a grinding of pepper. Serve right away.

TURKEY & CABBAGE SOUP

Prep time: **10 minutes** | Cook time: **40 minutes** | Serves **4**

- 2 tbsp olive oil
- ½ lb turkey breast, cubed
- 2 leeks, sliced
- 4 spring onions, chopped
- 2 cups green cabbage, grated
- 4 celery sticks, chopped
- 4 cups vegetable stock
- ½ tsp sweet paprika
- ½ tsp ground nutmeg
- 1 carrot, peeled
- Salt and black pepper to taste

1. Warm the olive oil in a pot over medium heat and brown turkey for 4 minutes, stirring occasionally.
2. Add in leeks, spring onions, carrot, and celery and cook for another minute.
3. Stir in cabbage, vegetable stock, sweet paprika, nutmeg, salt, and pepper and bring to a boil.
4. Cook for 30 minutes.
5. Serve.

SICILIAN ORANGE AND FENNEL SALAD

Prep time: **15 minutes** | Cook time: **none** | Serves **4 to 6**

- 2 navel oranges
- 1 bulb fennel
- ½ red onion
- 2 sprigs fresh mint leaves, finely chopped
- Extra-virgin olive oil, for drizzling
- Juice from 1 lemon
- 1 teaspoon honey
- Salt

1. Peel the oranges. Cut them into ½-inch slices, across the segment grain. Then quarter each slice. Remove any seeds.
2. Trim off the long stems from the fennel bulb. Trim the root end. Cut off the tough outer layer. Cut remaining fennel bulb lengthwise in quarters. Cut each quarter lengthwise into very thin slices. Cut the red onion into thin, half-moon slices.
3. Combine the oranges, fennel, onion, and mint in a large serving bowl. Drizzle a little olive oil to coat. In a small bowl, mix together the lemon juice and honey. Drizzle this dressing over the salad and season with salt to taste. Toss well and serve.

PRAWN SOUP

Prep time: **10 minutes** | Cook time: **15 minutes** | Serves **4**

- 1 lb prawns, peeled and deveined
- 3 tbsp olive oil
- 1 cucumber, chopped
- 3 cups tomato juice
- 3 roasted red peppers, chopped
- 2 tbsp balsamic vinegar
- 1 garlic clove, minced
- Salt and black pepper to taste
- ½ tsp cumin
- 1 tsp thyme, chopped

1. In a food processor or a blender, blitz tomato juice, cucumber, red peppers, 2 tbsp of olive oil, vinegar, cumin, salt, pepper, and garlic until smooth.
2. Remove to a bowl and transfer to the fridge for 10 minutes.
3. Warm the remaining oil in a pot over medium heat and sauté prawns, salt, pepper, and thyme for 4 minutes on all sides; then let them cool.
4. Ladle the soup into individual bowls and serve topped with prawns.

PEAR & ENDIVE SALAD

Prep time: **10 minutes** | Cook time: **5 minutes** | Serves **4**

- 2 tbsp olive oil
- 1 tbsp balsamic vinegar
- 2 garlic cloves, minced
- 1 tsp yellow mustard
- 1 tbsp lemon juice
- Sea salt and pepper to taste
- 12 black olives, chopped
- 1 tbsp parsley, chopped
- 7 cups baby spinach
- 2 endives, shredded
- 2 pears, sliced lengthwise
- 2 fennel bulbs, shredded

1. Place the spinach, endives, pears, fennel, parsley, olives, salt, pepper, lemon juice, olive oil, mustard, garlic, and balsamic vinegar in a bowl and toss to combine.
2. Serve right away.

PANZANELLA SALAD WITH CUCUMBERS

Prep time: **15 minutes** | Cook time: **none** | Serves **4 to 6**

- 2 cucumbers
- 3 or 4 sprigs mint, leaves removed, stems discarded
- 3 or 4 large, ripe tomatoes, cut into thin wedges
- 1 small red onion, cut into thin half-moons
- 1 loaf day-old (slightly stale) Italian bread, torn into bite-size pieces
- ⅓ cup olive oil
- ⅓ cup vinegar
- Salt
- Freshly ground black pepper

1. Trim the cucumber ends, and slice cucumbers in half lengthwise. Then cut in thick half-moons. Tear mint leaves into small pieces. Toss cucumbers, mint, tomatoes, onion, and bread together in a large mixing bowl.
2. Dress with   cup each olive oil and vinegar. Season with salt and pepper to taste. Let salad sit for 15 to 30 minutes so the bread can absorb the juices and soften a bit before serving.

GARDEN SALAD

Prep time: **10 minutes** | Cook time: **10 minutes** | Serves **4**

- ¼ cup extra-virgin olive oil
- 2 green onions, sliced
- ½ tsp fresh lemon zest
- 3 tbsp balsamic vinegar
- Salt to taste
- 2 cups baby spinach
- 1 cup watercress
- 1 cup arugula
- 1 celery stick, sliced

1. In a bowl, whisk together the lemon zest, balsamic vinegar, olive oil, and salt.
2. Put the remaining ingredients in a large bowl.
3. Pour the dressing over the salad and lightly toss to coat.
4. Serve and enjoy!

FIG & PROSCIUTTO SALAD

Prep time: **10 minutes** | Cook time: **15 minutes** | Serves **2**

- 2 tbsp crumbled Gorgonzola cheese
- 2 tbsp olive oil
- 3 cups Romaine lettuce, torn
- 4 figs, sliced
- 3 thin prosciutto slices
- ¼ cup pecan halves, toasted
- 1 tbsp balsamic vinegar

1. Toss the lettuce and figs in a large bowl.
2. Drizzle with olive oil.
3. Slice the prosciutto lengthwise into 1-inch strips.
4. Add the prosciutto, pecans, and Gorgonzola cheese to the bowl.
5. Toss the salad lightly.
6. Drizzle with balsamic vinegar.

POTATO AND GREEN PEA SOUP

Prep time: **10 minutes** | Cook time: **25 minutes** | Serves **4-6**

- 2 tablespoons butter
- 2 tablespoons vegetable oil
- 3 cups onion cut into very thin slices
- salt
- 2 garlic cloves, peeled and cut into paper-thin slices
- 3 cups potatoes, peeled and cut into very, very fine dice
- Basic Homemade Meat Broth, prepared as directed on , enough to cover all ingredients by 2 inches, or 1 beef bouillon cube
- 2 pounds fresh peas, unshelled weight, or 1 ten-ounce package frozen peas, thawed
- black pepper, ground fresh from the mill
- freshly grated parmigiano-reggiano cheese for the table

1. Choose a saucepan that can subsequently contain all the ingredients comfortably, put in the butter, oil, sliced onion, and a large pinch of salt, turn the heat on to low, and cover the pan. Cook the onion, turning it occasionally, until it becomes very soft and has shed all its liquid. Then uncover the pan, turn up the heat to medium, and cook, stirring once or twice, until all the liquid has bubbled away and the onion has become colored a tawny gold.

2. Add the sliced garlic and cook, stirring once or twice, until it becomes colored a pale gold. Add the potato dice, turning them several times during a minute or two to coat them well, then add enough broth to cover by 2 inches, or equivalent quantity of water together with a bouillon cube. Turn the heat down to cook at a slow, steady simmer, cover the pan, and cook for about 30 minutes.

3. Add the shelled fresh peas or thawed ones. If using fresh peas, cook another 10 minutes or more until they are done, replenishing the liquid if it falls below the original level. (Expect a substantial quantity of the fine potato dice to dissolve.) If using frozen peas, cook until they lose their raw taste, about 4 or 5 minutes. Taste and correct for salt. Add a few grindings of pepper, stir, and serve at once, with grated Parmesan on the side.

FARRO AND CHICKPEA SOUP

Prep time: **10 minutes** | Cook time: **1 hour 40 minutes** | Serves **6**

- 1 pound dried chickpeas
- 2 ounces pancetta, cut into chunks
- 4 garlic cloves, crushed and peeled
- 1 tablespoon fresh rosemary leaves
- 1 tablespoon fresh sage leaves
- 5 tablespoons extra-virgin olive oil, plus more for drizzling
- 1 large onion, cut into chunks
- 2 large carrots, peeled and cut into chunks
- 2 celery stalks, cut into chunks
- One 28-ounce can whole San Marzano tomatoes, crushed by hand
- 2 fresh bay leaves
- 1 tablespoon kosher salt
- ¼ teaspoon crushed red pepper flakes
- 1½ cups farro

1. Put the chickpeas in a bowl with water to cover by several inches. Refrigerate and soak overnight. Rinse and drain.

2. In a food processor, combine the pancetta, garlic, rosemary, and sage. Process to make a smooth paste or pestata.

3. Heat a large Dutch oven over medium-high heat. Add the olive oil. When the oil is hot, add the pestata and cook to render the fat from the pancetta, about 5 minutes.

4. Meanwhile, in the same food-processor work bowl, combine the onion, carrots, and celery, and process to make a second smooth pestata. Add to the pot and cook, stirring occasionally, until mixture dries out and begins to stick to the bottom of the pot, about 10 minutes.

5. Add the tomatoes, slosh out the can with water, and add that as well. Add 5 quarts water, the drained chickpeas, and the bay leaves. Bring to a boil, uncovered, and simmer rapidly until chickpeas are tender but not falling apart and soup has reduced by about a third and thickened, about 1 hour to 1 hour and 15 minutes, depending on the age of your chickpeas.

6. Add the salt, red pepper flakes, and farro, and simmer until just tender, about 20 to 25 minutes. Remove bay leaves. Serve soup drizzled with olive oil.

CHAPTER 5: PASTA AND PIZZA

ITALIAN SAUSAGE PIZZA WRAPS

Prep time: **10 minutes** | Cook time: **20 minutes** | Serves **2**

- 1 tbsp basil, chopped
- 1 tsp olive oil
- 6 oz spicy Italian sausage
- 1 shallot, chopped
- 1 tsp Italian seasoning
- 4 oz marinara sauce
- 2 flour tortillas
- ½ cup mozzarella, shredded
- 1/3 cup Parmesan, grated
- 1 tsp red pepper flakes

1. Warm olive oil in a skillet over medium heat.
2. Add and cook the sausage for 5-6 minutes, stirring and breaking up larger pieces, until cooked through.
3. Remove to a bowl.
4. Sauté the shallot for 3 minutes until soft, stirring frequently.
5. Stir in Italian seasoning, marinara sauce, and reserved sausage.
6. Bring to a simmer and cook for about 2 minutes.
7. Divide the mixture between the tortillas, top with the cheeses, add red pepper flakes and basil, and fold over.
8. Serve.

LINGUINE WITH CLAM SAUCE

Prep time: **10 minutes** | Cook time: **2 minutes** | Serves **6**

- 1 pound linguine
- 1/2 cup plus 1 tablespoon olive oil
- 6 cloves garlic, finely chopped
- 1/4 cup dry white wine
- 18 littleneck or chowder clams
- Kosher salt and freshly ground black pepper
- 1 tablespoon chopped fresh Italian, flat leafed parsley

1. Bring a large pot of salted water to a boil and cook the pasta, following the package instructions, until al dente.
2. Meanwhile, warm 1/2 cup of the olive oil in a high-sided saucepan set over medium-high heat. Add the garlic and cook until softened, about 2 minutes. Add the wine and allow it to cook away slightly, about 1 minute. Add the clams and their juice, and season with salt and pepper. Cook until the broth froths to a level of 1 to 2 inches. Remove from the heat. Stir in the parsley.
3. Drain the pasta and toss in a serving bowl with the remaining 1 tablespoon olive oil. Distribute evenly among six dinner plates. Top with equal portions of the sauce, and serve immediately.

FARFALLE WITH WHITE VODKA SAUCE

Prep time: 10 minutes | Cook time: 35 minutes | Serves 4 to 6

- ¾ cup (1½ sticks) unsalted butter
- 2½ cups thinly sliced yellow onions (about 2 medium)
- 1½ cups thinly sliced shallots (3 to 4 medium)
- 1 tablespoon plus 2 teaspoons kosher salt, plus more for the pasta water
- ¼ teaspoon ground white pepper
- ½ cup vodka

- 1 cup vegetable stock or unsalted chicken stock, store-bought or homemade
- 1 cup crème fraîche
- ½ cup finely grated parmigiano-reggiano cheese
- farfalle or 1 pound store-bought dried farfalle

1. In a medium pot, melt 8 tablespoons (1 stick) of the butter over medium heat. Add the onions, shallots, salt, and white pepper and stir well to combine. Cook, stirring often, until the onions release their liquid and wilt, 10 to 12 minutes.

2. Add the vodka, increase the heat to high, and continue to cook, stirring often, until the alcohol is evaporated, about 4 minutes. Add the stock and continue to cook, stirring often, until the onions are very translucent and soft and the liquid is fully evaporated, another 7 to 9 minutes.

3. Carefully transfer the onion mixture to a blender along with the crème fraîche and parmesan. Open the steam vent in the blender lid and cover the opening with a towel to avoid hot splatter and blend on high until very smooth, about 3 minutes.

4. In a large pot, bring 4 quarts water and ½ cup kosher salt to a boil over high heat. Add the farfalle and cook the fresh pasta until the ends are soft and the middle is just cooked through, about 1 minute 30 seconds; for dried, cook according to the package directions. Drain and return to the cooking pot. Add the pureed sauce from the blender and heat over medium-high until the sauce bubbles; it should thicken and coat the pasta in an even layer. Add the remaining 4 tablespoons butter and stir until melted and velvety.

5. Serve immediately in individual bowls or family style. Leftover pasta keeps, tightly covered in the refrigerator, for up to 3 days. Reheat over low heat, stirring in 1 to 2 tablespoons of water or stock to loosen the sauce if necessary.

PIZZA MARGHERITA

Prep time: 10 minutes | Cook time: 10 minutes | Serves 2

- 1 batch pizza dough
- ½ to ¾ cup Marinara Sauce

- 4 ounces fresh mozzarella, thinly sliced
- 1 tablespoon extra-virgin olive oil

6. Preheat oven to 450 degrees F. Place a pizza stone on the rack in the lower third of the oven. (You can use a sheet pan or a 10-inch cast-iron skillet to bake the pizza if you do not have a stone.)

7. Divide the dough in half, then form each half into a flat round and let rest on top of your knuckles on both raised fists. Use your knuckles to pull out and stretch the round into a thin circle. Place the dough circle on your work surface, and press it out as thin as you can with your fingertips.

8. Place the dough circle on a piece of parchment on a pizza peel-paddle (or, if you do not have a pizza paddle, slide the parchment paper with the pizza-dough circle onto the back of a sheet pan). Spread half of the sauce on the dough, using just enough sauce to dot about half of the pizza's surface, leaving a lip around the edge. In the spaces where you haven't dotted sauce, lay half of the cheese. Drizzle with half of the olive oil. Slide off the pizza peel or sheet pan onto the baking stone (or onto your cast-iron skillet).

9. Bake the pizza until the cheese is melted and bubbly and the crust is browned and crisp on the bottom, about 10 minutes. Remove from oven, and repeat with remaining dough, sauce, cheese, and olive oil.

ASPARAGUS & MOZZARELLA PASTA

Prep time: **10 minutes** | Cook time: **40 minutes** | Serves **4**

- 1 ½ lb asparagus, cut into 1-inch
- 2 tbsp olive oil
- 8 oz orecchiette
- 2 cups cherry tomatoes, halved
- Salt and black pepper to taste
- 2 cups fresh mozzarella, chopped
- ⅓ cup torn basil leaves
- 2 tbsp balsamic vinegar

1. Preheat oven to 390 F.
2. In a large pot, cook the pasta according to the directions.
3. Drain, reserving ¼ cup of cooking water.
4. In the meantime, in a large bowl, toss in asparagus, cherry tomatoes, oil, pepper, and salt.
5. Spread the mixture onto a rimmed baking sheet and bake for 15 minutes, stirring twice throughout cooking.
6. Remove the veggies from the oven, and add the cooked pasta to the baking sheet.
7. Mix with a few tbsp of pasta water to smooth the sauce and veggies.
8. Slowly mix in the mozzarella and basil.
9. Drizzle with the balsamic vinegar and serve in bowls.

FUSILLI WITH RED WINE AND PANCETTA

Prep time: **10 minutes** | Cook time: **15 minutes** | Serves **4 to 6**

- 2 tablespoons extra-virgin olive oil
- ¼ pound pancetta, diced
- Salt
- 1 pound cut pasta, such as fusilli or corkscrew shape
- 1 cup Chianti wine or favorite dry red wine
- Freshly ground black pepper
- ½ cup grated Parmesan or pecorino or combination
- 8 to 10 fresh sage leaves, diced

1. In a pasta pot or large saucepan, bring 4 quarts of water to a boil.
2. Meanwhile, place the olive oil and chopped pancetta in a small frying pan. Cook until the pancetta is lightly browned, about 5 minutes. Remove from the heat and set aside.
3. Add 1 tablespoon salt to the boiling water, then stir in the pasta and cook until it is almost done, just before al dente (the pasta will cook some more in the wine).
4. Meanwhile, pour the wine into a large, deep sauté pan and bring it to a simmer over medium heat. Add a pinch of salt. When the pasta is almost done cooking, use a skimmer or strainer to scoop the pasta out of the pot, and drop it into the simmering wine. Let the pasta cook at a lively simmer, stirring frequently, for about 2 minutes or until the wine is mostly or completely absorbed. Season with salt and pepper.
5. Scrape the pancetta and its oil into the pan with the pasta, stir in the cheese and sage leaves, and season with salt and pepper to taste. Serve hot.

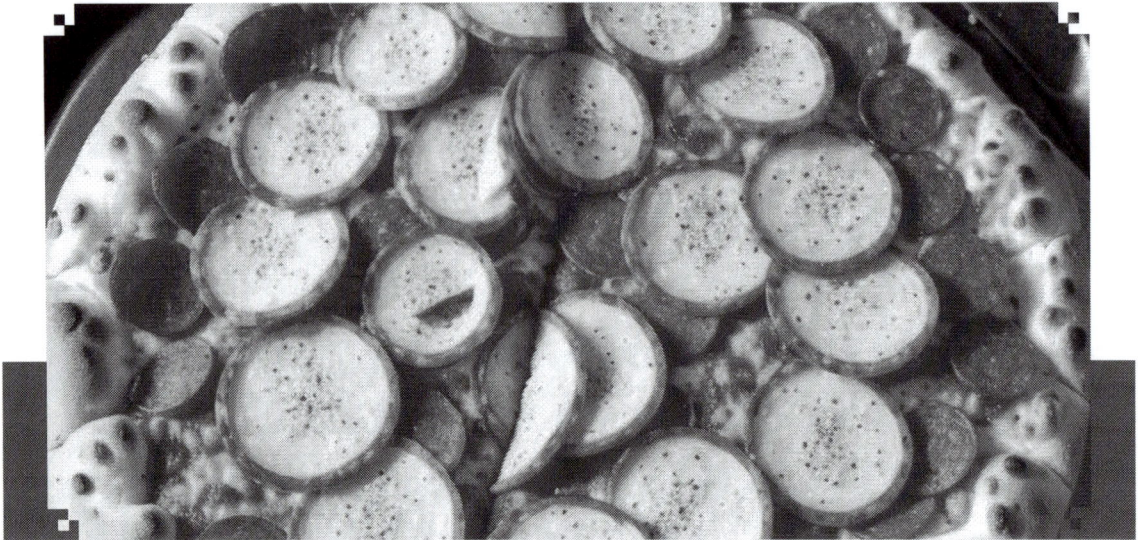

EASY SALAMI PIZZA

Prep time: 10 minutes | Cook time: 45 minutes | Serves 4

- For The Crust
- 2 tbsp olive oil
- 2 cups flour
- 1 cup lukewarm water
- 1 pinch of sugar
- 1 tsp active dry yeast
- ¾ tsp salt
- For The Topping

- 1 cup sliced smoked mozzarella cheese
- 1 tbsp olive oil
- 1 cup sliced salami
- ¼ cup marinara sauce
- ¼ bell pepper, sliced
- ¼ red onion, thinly sliced

1. Sift flour and salt in a bowl and stir in yeast.
2. Mix lukewarm water, olive oil, and sugar in another bowl.
3. Add the wet mixture to the dry mixture and whisk until you obtain a soft dough.
4. Place the dough on a lightly floured work surface and knead it thoroughly for 4-5 minutes until elastic.
5. Transfer the dough to a greased bowl.
6. Cover with cling film and leave to rise for 50-60 minutes in a warm place until doubled in size.
7. Roll out the dough to a thickness of around 12 inches.
8. Preheat the oven to 400 F.
9. Line a pizza pan with parchment paper.
10. Heat the olive oil and cook the salami until brown, 5 minutes.
11. Spread the marinara sauce on the crust, and top with the mozzarella cheese, salami, bell pepper, and onion.
12. Bake in the oven until the cheese melts, 15 minutes.
13. Remove it from the oven, slice, and serve warm.

PASTA WITH 15-MINUTE TOMATO SAUCE

Prep time: **5 minutes** | Cook time: **15 minutes** | Serves **4 to 6**

- 2 tablespoons extra-virgin olive oil
- 1 medium onion, finely diced
- ¼ cup dry white wine
- 1 (28-ounce) can crushed tomatoes
- Salt
- Freshly ground black pepper
- 1 pound pasta

1. Heat 4 quarts of water in a pasta pot or large saucepan.
2. Heat oil in a medium saucepan. When hot, add onion. Cook on medium to medium-high heat for about 3 to 5 minutes until onion has softened.
3. Add the wine. Let the wine evaporate to about half its volume.
4. Add tomatoes. Season lightly with salt and pepper. Let simmer for 10 to 15 minutes.
5. When pasta water is boiling, add 1 tablespoon salt. Add pasta. Cook to al dente. Drain.
6. Add pasta to a large serving bowl. Coat with tomato sauce.

PASTA PRIMAVERA

Prep time: **10 minutes** | Cook time: **25 minutes** | Serves **4**

- ½ cup grated Pecorino Romano
- 2 cups cauliflower florets, chopped
- ¼ cup olive oil
- 16 oz tortiglioni
- ½ cup chopped green onions
- 1 red bell pepper, sliced
- 4 garlic cloves, minced
- 1 cup grape tomatoes, halved
- 2 tsp dried Italian seasoning
- ½ lemon, juiced

1. In a large pot of boiling water, cook the tortiglioni pasta for 8-10 minutes until al dente.
2. Drain and set aside.
3. Heat olive oil in a skillet and sauté onion, cauliflower, and bell pepper for 7 minutes.
4. Mix in garlic and cook until fragrant, 30 seconds.
5. Stir in the tomatoes and Italian seasoning; cook until the tomatoes soften, 5 minutes.
6. Mix in the lemon juice and tortiglioni.
7. Garnish with cheese.

LASAGNE WITH RICOTTA PESTO

Prep time: **10 minutes** | Cook time: **35 minutes** | Serves **6**

- 2 tablespoons salt
- 1 tablespoon extra virgin olive oil
- freshly grated parmigiano-reggiano cheese at the table

1. Make yellow pasta dough either by the machine method, , or by the hand-rolled method. Cut the dough into rectangular strips about 3½ inches wide and 5 inches long. Spread them out on a counter lined with clean, dry, cloth towels.
2. Make the ricotta pesto, following the directions on .
3. Bring 4 to 5 quarts water to a boil. Add 2 tablespoons salt and 1 tablespoon olive oil. As the water returns to a boil, put in half the pasta. (It's not advisable to put it all in at one time, because the broad strips may stick to each other.)
4. As soon as the first batch of pasta is done al dente, retrieve it with a colander spoon or skimmer, and spread it out on a warm serving platter. Take a spoonful of hot water from the pasta pot and use it to thin out the pesto. Spread half the pesto over the pasta in the platter.
5. Drop the remaining pasta into the pot, drain it when done, spread it on the platter over the previous layer of pasta, cover with the remaining pesto, and serve at once with grated Parmesan on the side.

PASTA WITH 30-MINUTE MEAT SAUCE

Prep time: **10 minutes** | Cook time: **30 minutes** | Serves **4 to 5**

- 2 tablespoons extra-virgin olive oil
- 1 medium onion, finely diced
- 2 garlic cloves, peeled and smashed
- ½ pound ground beef
- ⅓ cup dry white wine
- 1 (28-ounce) can crushed tomatoes
- Salt
- Freshly ground black pepper
- 1 pound pasta
- ½ cup grated Parmesan for servings

1. Heat oil in a medium saucepan. Add onion and garlic. Cook on medium heat until onion softens, about 3 to 4 minutes.
2. Add beef. Brown meat, breaking up into smaller pieces, leaving some larger chunks (making for a rustic mixture of meat pieces). When the meat is no longer pink, add the wine. Let it sizzle and mostly evaporate.
3. Add the can of tomatoes. Season with salt and pepper. Stir to combine. Simmer for 20 minutes, cover askew.
4. Heat 4 quarts of water in a pasta pot or large saucepan. When boiling, salt the water. Add the pasta. Cook until al dente. When done, drain. Add to a large serving bowl. Spoon on some sauce and gently coat. You can add extra sauce on top of individual servings, and pass around grated Parmesan.

FRIED MINI PIZZAS

Prep time: **10 minutes** | Cook time: **5 minutes** | Serves 3 to 4

- 2 cups all-purpose flour
- 1 teaspoon salt
- 1 tablespoon olive oil
- 1 teaspoon rapid-rise yeast
- ¼ to ¾ cup warm water
- Olive oil, for greasing
- Vegetable oil, for frying
- Rosemary leaves
- Sea salt
- Grated Parmesan cheese

1. On a clean surface, create a mound with the flour. Add the salt, olive oil, and yeast, and mix. Slowly add some warm water, anywhere from ¼ to ¾ cup, until a soft, elastic dough is formed. Knead for several minutes.
2. Place the dough in an oiled bowl, cover, and allow to rise until doubled in size, 1½ to 2 hours.
3. When doubled, pull small balls of dough, and use a rolling pin or your hands to shape the dough into very small pizzas. It's perfectly acceptable (in fact, desired) for the pizzas to have an odd shape and not be perfectly round.
4. Heat the vegetable oil to 350°F. Plunge the pizzette in the hot oil, and brown them on both sides for several minutes. Remove from the oil, place on paper towels, and top with rosemary leaves, sea salt, and cheese.

PEPPER-BROCCOLI PIZZA

Prep time: **10 minutes** | Cook time: **25 minutes** | Serves **4**

- For The Crust
- 1 tbsp olive oil
- ½ cup almond flour
- ¼ tsp salt
- 2 tbsp ground psyllium husk
- 1 cup lukewarm water
- For The Topping
- 1 tbsp olive oil
- 1 cup sliced fresh mushrooms
- 1 white onion, thinly sliced
- 3 cups broccoli florets
- 4 garlic cloves, minced
- ½ cup pizza sauce
- 4 tomatoes, sliced
- 1 ½ cups grated mozzarella
- ½ cup grated Parmesan cheese

1. Preheat oven to 400 F.
2. Line a baking sheet with parchment paper.
3. In a bowl, mix the almond flour, salt, psyllium powder, olive oil, and lukewarm water until the dough forms.
4. Spread the mixture on the pizza pan and bake in the oven until crusty, 10 minutes.
5. Remove and allow cooling.
6. Heat olive oil in a skillet and sauté the mushrooms, onion, garlic, and broccoli until softened, 5 minutes.
7. Spread the pizza sauce on the crust and top with the broccoli mixture, tomato, mozzarella and Parmesan.
8. Bake for 5 minutes.

LINGUINE WITH "ANGRY LOBSTER"

Prep time: **10 minutes** | Cook time: **20 minutes** | Serves **4**

- 2 fresh lobsters (about 11/2 pounds each)
- 1 pound linguine
- 2/3 cup extra virgin olive oil
- 1/3 cup minced shallots
- 1/4 cup minced garlic
- 1/2 cup chopped fresh Italian, flat leafed parsley
- 1/3 cup chopped fresh basil leaves
- 1 teaspoon red pepper flakes
- Kosher salt and freshly ground black pepper
- 1/2 cup dry white wine
- 1 cup chopped canned tomatoes (with some of the juice)

1. Bring a large pot of water to a boil. Add the lobsters, cover, and cook until the shells are bright red, about 15 minutes. Drain and set aside to cool.
2. Separate the claws from the body and extract the claw meat. Set aside. Cut the lobsters in half lengthwise. Remove the tail meat and roe. Chop the tail and claw meat into bite-size pieces and set aside. Finely chop the roe and set aside. Discard the green tomalley, and rinse the shells thoroughly under cold running water. Reserve the shells until ready to serve.
3. Bring a large pot of salted water to a boil. Add the linguine and cook until al dente, following the package instructions. Reserve 1/2 cup of the pasta cooking water before draining.
4. Warm 1/3 cup of the olive oil in a large saucepan set over medium-high heat. Add the shallots and cook to flavor the oil, stirring frequently, about 30 seconds. Stir in the garlic, 1/4 cup of the parsley, half the basil, and the red pepper flakes. Cook to soften the garlic slightly, about 2 minutes. Add three quarters of the lobster meat and all of the roe. Cook, stirring frequently, to flavor the lobster with the aromatics, about 2 minutes. Season with salt and pepper. Add the wine and bring to a boil. Add the tomatoes and simmer, stirring frequently. Stir in the remaining lobster meat. Add the drained pasta, the remaining 1/4 cup parsley, the remaining basil, and the remaining 1/3 cup olive oil. Toss to coat the pasta with the sauce. If the pasta seems dry, add the reserved pasta water. Spoon onto plates and serve immediately.

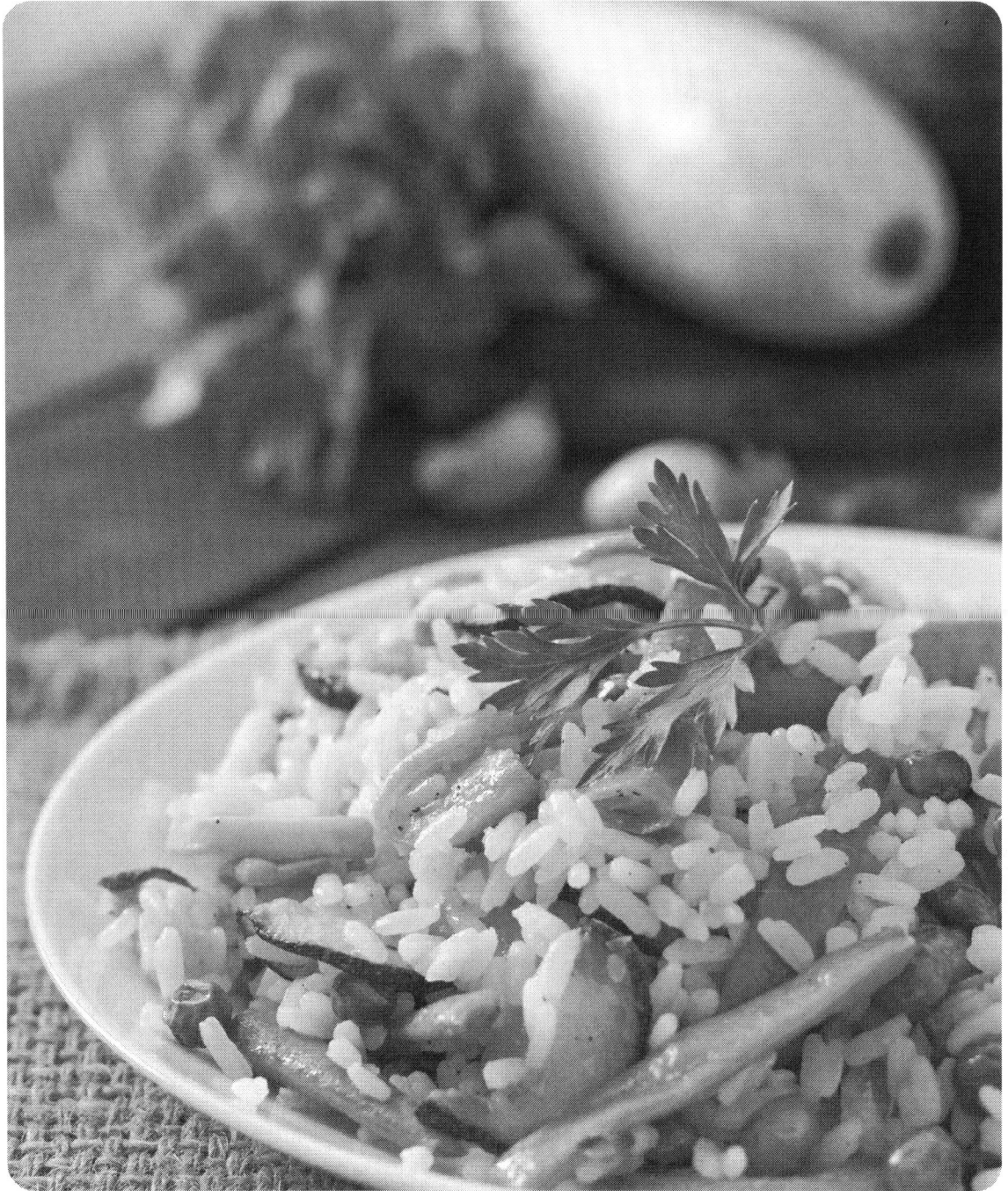

CHAPTER 6: BEANS, RICE AND GRAINS

OLIVE GREEN RICE

Prep time: 10 minutes | Cook time: 35 minutes | Serves 4

- 2 tbsp butter
- 4 spring onions, sliced
- 1 leek, sliced
- 1 medium zucchini, chopped
- 5 oz broccoli florets
- 2 oz curly kale
- ½ cup frozen green peas
- 2 cloves garlic, minced
- 1 thyme sprig, chopped
- 1 rosemary sprig, chopped
- 1 cup white rice
- 2 cups vegetable broth
- 1 large tomato, chopped
- 2 oz black olives, sliced

1. In a saucepan, melt the butter over medium heat.
2. Cook the spring onions, leek, and zucchini for 4-5 minutes or until tender.
3. Add in the garlic, thyme, and rosemary and continue to sauté for about 1 minute or until aromatic.
4. Add in the rice, broth, and tomato.
5. Bring to a boil, turn the heat to a gentle simmer, and cook for about 10-12 minutes.
6. Stir in broccoli, kale, and green peas, and continue cooking for 5 minutes.
7. Fluff the rice with a fork and garnish with olives.

CAVOLO NERO FARRO PILAF

Prep time: 10 minutes | Cook time: 50 minutes | Serves 4

- 2 tbsp olive oil
- 1 cup green peas
- 4 cups cavolo nero, torn
- ½ cup hummus
- ½ cup scallions, sliced
- 1 garlic clove, minced
- 1 cup farro
- 2 cups water
- 1 cup chopped tomatoes
- 1 tbsp tomato paste
- 1 tsp cumin
- ½ tsp oregano
- 2 tbsp fresh cilantro, chopped
- Salt and black pepper to taste

1. Heat olive oil in a skillet over medium heat.
2. Add in scallions, sauté until tender.
3. Add in garlic, cumin, and oregano and cook for another 30 seconds.
4. Stir in farro, water, chopped tomatoes, and tomato paste.
5. Bring to a boil, then lower the heat, and simmer for 30-40 minutes.
6. Stir in peas, cavolo nero, salt, and black pepper.
7. Let sit covered for 8 minutes.
8. Serve topped with hummus and cilantro.

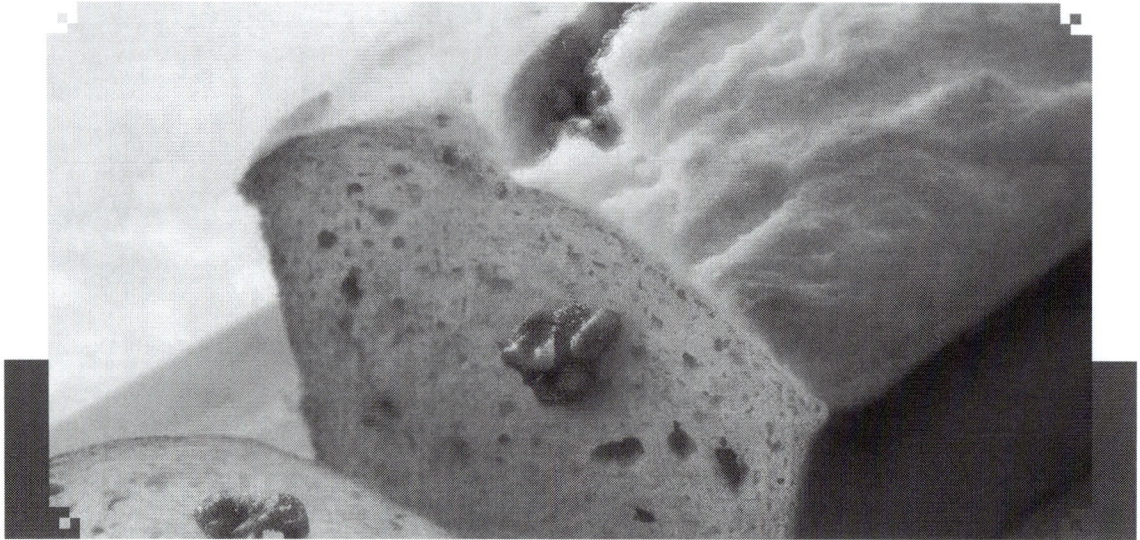

WALNUT BREAD

Prep time: 10 minutes | Cook time: 1 hour 33 minutes | Serves 8

- 2½ cups warm water
- 1 package dry yeast
- 6 cups whole wheat flour, or more as needed
- 1 teaspoon kosher salt
- ⅓ cup whole milk powder
- 3 tablespoons honey
- ¼ cup olive oil
- ½ cup walnut oil
- 1½ cups coarsely chopped walnuts

1. In a small bowl, stir 1/4 cup of the warm water and the yeast. Set aside for 5 minutes.
2. In a large bowl, toss 3 cups of the flour, the salt, and the milk powder. Stir in the yeast mixture along with the remaining 21/4 cups warm water, the honey, olive oil, and walnut oil. Mix with a fork or the dough hook of a stand mixer until well combined. Add the walnuts and 1 cup of the remaining flour to the mixture, kneading to combine. Continue adding the remaining 2 cups flour, 1/4 cup at a time, until the dough is moist and slightly sticky. Set aside to rest for 5 minutes.
3. Turn the dough out onto a lightly floured surface. Knead until the dough is soft and elastic, about 8 minutes. If the dough is very sticky, add more flour, 1/4 cup at a time, while kneading.
4. Place the dough in a clean bowl and cover with plastic wrap and a clean dish towel. Set aside in a warm place and allow to rise for 1 hour.
5. Preheat the oven to 375° F. Line two baking sheets with parchment paper and set aside.
6. Divide the risen dough in half and shape each half into a round loaf. Place on baking sheets and cover with a dish towel. Set aside and allow to double in size, about 40 minutes.
7. Bake the loaves until they are deep golden brown and firm, 40 to 45 minutes.

RISOTTO WITH VEGETABLES

Prep time: **10 minutes** | Cook time: **46 minutes** | Serves **6**

- ½ pound broccoli (about 1 medium-size stalk)
- 1 cup blanched fava beans or frozen baby lima beans
- ½ teaspoon salt, plus more as needed
- 3 tablespoons extra-virgin olive oil
- ½ cup minced scallions, greens included (about 6)
- 1 tablespoon minced shallot
- 2½ cups Arborio or Carnaroli rice
- ½ cup dry white wine
- 6½ cups hot vegetable stock or chicken broth
- 2 tablespoons unsalted butter, cut into bits
- ½ cup freshly grated Grana Padano, Parmigiano-Reggiano, or Pecorino Romano cheese
- Freshly ground black pepper to taste

1. Trim the broccoli florets from the stems, keeping them small enough to fit on a spoon. (You should have about 1¼ cups.) Peel the stems with a small knife or vegetable peeler, then cut them into 2-inch pieces. Steam the florets just until bright green, about 1 minute. Steam the stems until very tender, about 4 minutes. Reserve the steaming liquid. Transfer the stems to a blender or food processor, and process until smooth. You will probably have to add some of the steaming liquid to make a smooth mixture. Scrape out the purée into a small bowl, and set the florets and purée aside.
2. If using the baby lima beans, cook them in a small saucepan of boiling salted water for 2 minutes. Drain them thoroughly and set aside.
3. Heat the olive oil in a heavy casserole or pot over medium heat. Add the scallions and shallot and sauté until translucent, stirring often, about 4 minutes. Add the rice, and stir to coat with the oil. Toast the rice until the edges become translucent, 1 to 2 minutes.
4. Pour in the wine, and stir well until evaporated. Add ½ cup of the hot stock and the ½ teaspoon salt. Cook, stirring constantly, until all the stock has been absorbed. Continue to add hot stock in small batches—just enough to completely moisten the rice—and cook until each successive batch has been absorbed. After the risotto has cooked for 12 minutes, stir in the broccoli purée and the favas or limas. About 3 minutes after that, stir in the broccoli florets. Stir constantly, and adjust the level of heat so the rice is simmering very gently while adding the stock, until the rice mixture is creamy but al dente. This will take about 18 minutes from the first addition of stock.
5. Remove the casserole from the heat. Whip in the butter first, until melted, then the grated cheese. Adjust the seasoning with salt, if necessary, and pepper. Serve immediately, ladled into warm shallow bowls.

LAMB RISOTTO

Prep time: **10 minutes** | Cook time: **90 minutes** | Serves **4**

- 2 tbsp olive oil
- 2 garlic cloves, minced
- 1 onion, chopped
- 1 lb lamb, cubed
- Salt and black pepper to taste
- 2 cups vegetable stock
- 1 cup arborio rice
- 2 tbsp mint, chopped
- 1 cup Parmesan, grated

1. Warm olive oil in a skillet over medium heat and cook the onion for 5 minutes.
2. Put in lamb and cook for another 5 minutes.
3. Stir in garlic, salt, pepper, and stock and bring to a simmer; cook for 1 hour.
4. Stir in rice and cook for 18-20 minutes.
5. Top with Parmesan cheese and mint and serve.

SAUTÉED ARTICHOKES & FAVA BEANS

Prep time: **10 minutes** | Cook time: **50 minutes** | Serves **4**

- Juice of 2 lemons
- 4 large artichokes
- 2 tablespoons extra-virgin olive oil
- 4 oz (125 g) pancetta, cut into ¼-inch (6-mm) dice
- 2 cloves garlic, very thinly sliced
- ½ cup (4 fl oz/125 ml) dry white wine
- Fine sea salt and freshly ground black pepper
- 1 cup (5 oz/155 g) shelled, blanched, and peeled fava beans
- 2 tablespoons finely chopped fresh flat-leaf parsley

1. Fill a bowl with cold water and add the lemon juice. Cut the stems off the artichokes, trim the end and tough skin around the stem, and place in the lemon water. Cut off the top one-third from the artichokes and remove the tough outer leaves. Cut the artichokes in half lengthwise and scoop out the fuzzy chokes with a spoon. Cut them in half again and immerse the quarters in the lemon water.
2. In a heavy-bottomed sauté pan, heat the olive oil and pancetta over medium heat. Sauté until the pancetta is lightly crisped, about 10 minutes. Add the garlic, reduce the heat to medium-low, and sauté until the garlic is softened, about 5 minutes. Drain the artichokes, reserving ½ cup (4 fl oz/125 ml) of the lemon water. Add the artichokes to the pan along with the reserved water, the wine, ½ teaspoon salt, and a little pepper. Raise the heat to medium-high and bring to a boil. Return the heat to medium-low, cover, and cook until the artichokes are almost tender but still a little firm, 15–20 minutes.
3. Stir in the fava beans. Cover and cook until the fava beans are tender, about 10 minutes. Uncover, raise the heat to medium, and cook until most of the liquid has been absorbed, about 5 minutes longer. Remove from the heat and stir in the parsley. Transfer to a serving bowl, pour the pan juices over the top, and serve.

MARIA PIA'S EASTER BREAD

Prep time: **10 minutes** | Cook time: **30 minutes** | Serves **10**

- 9 large eggs, at room temperature
- 1/2 cup granulated sugar
- 1 teaspoon pure vanilla extract
- 4 cups all-purpose flour
- 1/2 teaspoon kosher salt
- 4 teaspoons baking powder
- 12 tablespoons (11/2 sticks) butter, softened
- 11/2 cups confectioners' sugar
- 2 tablespoons milk or water
- 1/2 teaspoon pure lemon extract

1. Preheat the oven to 350° F.
2. In a medium-size bowl, beat 6 of the eggs, the granulated sugar, and the vanilla until pale yellow and frothy. Set aside.
3. In a large bowl, stir together 3 cups of the flour, the salt, and the baking powder. Add the butter and blend with an electric mixer to form a crumbly mixture. Gradually beat in the egg mixture. Add up to 1/2 cup of the remaining flour to form a soft dough that is dry on the outside but still sticky on the inside.
4. Gently roll the dough into a log about 15 inches long and 2 inches in diameter. Cut off a 1-inch-long piece of the dough and set aside. Place the log on a baking sheet. Bring the ends of the log together to form a circle, pinching the dough together to seal the ends. Press 1 of the remaining eggs into the dough at this joint. Place the other 2 eggs an even distance apart on either side of the joint, gently pressing them into the dough.
5. Roll the reserved dough into six ropes about 1/2 inch wide and 4 inches long. Place two ropes over each egg to form an X, or cross, pinching gently to seal the ends of the ropes to the bread dough. Bake until the bread is light golden brown and a skewer inserted in the center comes out clean, about 30 minutes. Remove from the oven and allow to cool completely.
6. In a small bowl mix the confectioners' sugar, milk, and lemon extract, until smooth. Drizzle the icing back and forth over the bread to create a decorative topping. Allow the icing to set for 30 minutes before slicing and serving.

BROCCOLI AND GREEN BEANS

Prep time: 5 minutes | Cook time: 10 minutes | Makes 4 side-dish

- salt
- 8 cups of broccoli florets (about 2 pounds including the stems)
- ½ pound green beans, trimmed
- ½ cup extra-virgin olive oil
- 2 garlic cloves, thinly sliced
- 1½ teaspoons dried crushed red pepper flakes, plus more to taste
- ½ teaspoon sea salt, plus more to taste
- ½ teaspoon freshly ground black pepper, plus more to taste

1. Bring a large pot of salted water to a boil. Add the broccoli and cook just until the color brightens, about 2 minutes.
2. Using a slotted spoon, transfer the broccoli to a large bowl of ice water to cool completely.
3. Drain the broccoli and set aside.
4. Cook the green beans in the same pot of boiling salted water just until the color brightens, about 4 minutes.
5. Drain, then add the green beans to another large bowl of ice water to cool completely. (the vegetables can be prepared up to this point 8 hours ahead.
6. Dry thoroughly and refrigerate in a resealable plastic bag.)
7. In a large sauté pan, heat the oil over a medium-high flame.
8. When almost smoking, add the garlic and 1½ teaspoons of red pepper flakes, and sauté just until fragrant and the garlic is pale golden, about 45 seconds.
9. Using a slotted spoon, remove the garlic from the oil and discard (do not overcook the garlic as it will impart a very bitter taste to the dish). Add the broccoli, green beans, and ½ teaspoon each of sea salt and black pepper to the oil, and sauté until the vegetables are heated through and crisp-tender, about 5 minutes.
10. Season with more red pepper flakes, sea salt, and black pepper to taste.
11. Transfer the mixture to a bowl and serve immediately.

TARRAGON BUCKWHEAT

Prep time: 10 minutes | Cook time: 55 minutes | Serves 6

- 3 tbsp olive oil
- 1 ½ cups buckwheat, soaked
- 3 cups vegetable broth
- ½ onion, finely chopped
- 1 garlic clove, minced
- 2 tsp fresh tarragon, minced
- Salt and black pepper to taste
- 2 oz Parmesan cheese, grated
- 2 tbsp parsley, minced
- 2 tsp lemon juice

1. In your blender, pulse buckwheat until about half of the grains are broken into smaller pieces.
2. Bring broth and 3 cups of water to a boil in a medium saucepan over high heat.
3. Reduce heat to low, cover, and keep warm.
4. Warm 2 tablespoons oil in a pot over medium heat.
5. Add onion and cook until softened, 5 minutes.
6. Stir in garlic and cook until fragrant, about 30 seconds.
7. Add farro and cook, stirring frequently, until grains are lightly toasted, 3 minutes.
8. Stir 5 cups warm broth mixture into farro mixture, reduce heat to low, cover, and cook until almost all liquid has been absorbed and farro is just al dente, about 25 minutes, stirring twice during cooking.
9. Add tarragon, salt, and pepper and keep stirring for 5 minutes.
10. Remove from heat and stir in Parmesan cheese, parsley, lemon juice, and the remaining olive oil.
11. Adjust the seasoning and serve.

RISOTTO WITH VEGETABLES

Prep time: **10 minutes** | Cook time: **46 minutes** | Serves **6**

- ½ pound broccoli (about 1 medium-size stalk)
- 1 cup blanched fava beans or frozen baby lima beans
- ½ teaspoon salt, plus more as needed
- 3 tablespoons extra-virgin olive oil
- ½ cup minced scallions, greens included (about 6)
- 1 tablespoon minced shallot
- 2½ cups Arborio or Carnaroli rice
- ½ cup dry white wine
- 6½ cups hot vegetable stock or chicken broth
- 2 tablespoons unsalted butter, cut into bits
- ½ cup freshly grated Grana Padano, Parmigiano-Reggiano, or Pecorino Romano cheese
- Freshly ground black pepper to taste

1. Trim the broccoli florets from the stems, keeping them small enough to fit on a spoon. (You should have about 1¼ cups.) Peel the stems with a small knife or vegetable peeler, then cut them into 2-inch pieces. Steam the florets just until bright green, about 1 minute. Steam the stems until very tender, about 4 minutes. Reserve the steaming liquid. Transfer the stems to a blender or food processor, and process until smooth. You will probably have to add some of the steaming liquid to make a smooth mixture. Scrape out the purée into a small bowl, and set the florets and purée aside.

2. If using the baby lima beans, cook them in a small saucepan of boiling salted water for 2 minutes. Drain them thoroughly and set aside.

3. Heat the olive oil in a heavy casserole or pot over medium heat. Add the scallions and shallot and sauté until translucent, stirring often, about 4 minutes. Add the rice, and stir to coat with the oil. Toast the rice until the edges become translucent, 1 to 2 minutes.

4. 4.   Pour in the wine, and stir well until evaporated. Add ½ cup of the hot stock and the ½ teaspoon salt. Cook, stirring constantly, until all the stock has been absorbed. Continue to add hot stock in small batches—just enough to completely moisten the rice—and cook until each successive batch has been absorbed. After the risotto has cooked for 12 minutes, stir in the broccoli purée and the favas or limas. About 3 minutes after that, stir in the broccoli florets. Stir constantly, and adjust the level of heat so the rice is simmering very gently while adding the stock, until the rice mixture is creamy but al dente. This will take about 18 minutes from the first addition of stock.

5. Remove the casserole from the heat. Whip in the butter first, until melted, then the grated cheese. Adjust the seasoning with salt, if necessary, and pepper. Serve immediately, ladled into warm shallow bowls.

BROWN RICE & VEGETABLE LENTILS

Prep time: **10 minutes** | Cook time: **40 minutes** | Serves **4**

- 1 ½ tbsp olive oil
- 2 ¼ cups vegetable broth
- ½ cup green lentils
- ½ cup brown rice
- ½ cup diced carrots
- ½ cup diced celery
- 1 (2 ¼-oz) can olives, sliced
- ¼ cup diced red onion
- ¼ cup cilantro, chopped
- 1 tbsp lemon juice
- 1 garlic clove, minced
- Salt and black pepper to taste

1. In a large saucepan over high heat, bring the broth and lentils to a boil, cover, and lower the heat to medium-low.
2. Cook for 8 minutes.
3. Raise the heat to medium, and stir in the rice.
4. Cover the pot and cook the mixture for 14 minutes or until the liquid is absorbed.
5. Remove the pot from the heat and let sit covered for 2 minutes, then stir.
6. While the lentils and rice are cooking, combine carrots, celery, olives, onion, and cilantro in a serving bowl.
7. In a small bowl, whisk together the oil, lemon juice, garlic, salt, and black pepper.
8. Set aside.
9. Once the lentils and rice are done, add them to the serving bowl.
10. Pour the dressing on top, and mix well.
11. Serve warm.

RICE WITH FRESH SAGE

Prep time: **10 minutes** | Cook time: **20 minutes** | Serves **6**

- 4 tablespoons butter, plus 2 tablespoons butter cut into pieces for finishing
- 12 large fresh sage leaves
- 5 cups hot water or light stock, plus more if needed
- 2½ teaspoons kosher salt
- 2 cups Italian short-grain rice, such as Arborio or Carnaroli
- 1 bunch scallions, finely chopped (about 1 cup), for finishing
- ½ cup freshly grated Grana Padano or Parmigiano-Reggiano cheese, plus more for passing

1. Melt the 4 tablespoons butter in a saucepan over medium heat. When the butter is foaming, scatter the sage leaves in the pan and heat for a minute or so, just until they are sizzling. Pour in 5 cups of hot water or stock, and stir in the salt. Raise the heat, and bring the liquid to the boil; then stir in the rice and bring back to the boil.
2. Cover the pan, and lower the heat so the water is bubbling gently. Cook for 13 or 14 minutes, then check the rice and add more liquid if needed. At this point, too, stir in the scallions, to cook for the last minute or two, until the rice is creamy and al dente.
3. When the rice is fully cooked, turn off the heat, drop in the butter pieces, and stir vigorously until they have completely melted. Stir in the ½ cup of grated cheese, spoon the riso into warm pasta bowls, and serve immediately, passing additional grated cheese at the table.

CHAPTER 7:
POULTRY

ALMOND CHICKEN BALLS

Prep time: **10 minutes** | Cook time: **30 minutes** | Serves **4**

- 2 tbsp olive oil
- 1 lb ground chicken
- 2 tsp toasted chopped almonds
- 1 egg, whisked
- 2 tsp turmeric powder
- 2 garlic cloves, minced
- Salt and black pepper to taste
- 1 ¼ cups heavy cream
- ¼ cup parsley, chopped
- 1 tbsp chives, chopped

1. Place the ground chicken, almonds, egg, turmeric powder, garlic, salt, pepper, parsley, and chives in a bowl and toss to combine.
2. Form meatballs out of the mixture.
3. Warm olive oil in a skillet over medium heat.
4. Brown meatballs for 8 minutes on all sides.
5. Stir in cream and cook for another 10 minutes.

JUICY ALMOND TURKEY

Prep time: **10 minutes** | Cook time: **40 minutes** | Serves **4**

- 2 tbsp canola oil
- ¼ cup almonds, chopped
- 1 lb turkey breast, sliced
- Salt and black pepper to taste
- 1 lemon, juiced and zested
- 1 grapefruit, juiced
- 1 tbsp rosemary, chopped
- 3 garlic cloves, minced
- 1 cup chicken stock

1. Warm olive oil in a skillet over medium heat and cook garlic and turkey for 8 minutes on both sides.
2. Stir in salt, pepper, lemon juice, lemon zest, grapefruit juice, rosemary, almonds, and stock and bring to a boil.
3. Cook for 20 minutes.

ROASTED CALABRIAN CHICKEN

Prep time: **10 minutes** | Cook time: **30 minutes** | Serves **4**

- Nonstick cooking spray
- 8 boneless skinless chicken thighs
- 1 teaspoon salt
- 1 small onion, sliced
- 3 tablespoons olive oil
- 2 or 3 sprigs rosemary, leaves only
- 2 to 3 teaspoons dried oregano
- 2 or 3 medium potatoes, peeled and cubed
- 1 lemon, halved

1. Preheat the oven to 375°F, and move the oven rack to the second-lowest position. Coat a baking sheet with cooking spray or a few additional tablespoons of oil.
2. In a large mixing bowl, combine the chicken thighs, salt, onion, oil, rosemary, oregano, and potatoes, and mix well using clean hands or two wooden spoons.
3. Squeeze the lemon over all the ingredients.
4. Spread the ingredients on the baking sheet, and bake until the chicken is fully cooked, about 30 minutes.

DUCK WITH LEMON AND HONEY

Prep time: **10 minutes** | Cook time: **1 hour 45 minutes** | Serves **4**

- 2 teaspoons kosher salt
- 2 teaspoons fennel powder
- 2 tablespoons extra-virgin olive oil
- 6-pound duck, with gizzards, neck, and liver, trimmed of excess fat
- 2 sprigs fresh rosemary
- 1 large onion, quartered
- 3 cups Chicken Stock
- 1 cup dry red wine
- ¼ cup dried porcini mushrooms, crumbled
- 1 to 2 tablespoons honey
- Juice of ½ lemon, freshly squeezed

1. Preheat the oven to 375 degrees. In a small bowl, combine the salt and fennel powder. Drizzle in the olive oil, and stir to make a paste. Rub the salt paste all over the outside and inside of the duck. Stuff the cavity of the duck with the rosemary and the onion.

2. Chop the gizzards and liver, and put them in the bottom of a roasting pan along with the neck. Set a rack on top, and arrange the duck on the rack in the roasting pan, breast side up. Add the stock, wine, and porcini to the pan. Roast the duck until the skin is crispy, about 1 hour. Increase the oven temperature to 400 degrees, and cook for an additional ½ hour, until the skin is very crisp.

3. Remove the duck to a cutting board. Remove the rack, and set the roasting pan with the vegetables and sauce on top of the stove, over high heat. Boil until the cooking juices are reduced to about 2 cups. Strain them into a measuring cup (preferably a fat-separating measuring cup), pressing on the solids to get the juices out. Let the juices sit for a minute to separate the fat, and spoon or pour it off. Pour the defatted juices into a skillet, and bring them to a simmer over medium-high heat. Add the honey, to taste, and the lemon juice, and give it a 5-minute boil.

4. Cut the duck into four portions with kitchen shears, and place it, skin side up, in the roasting pan. Baste with some of the sauce, and return it to the 400-degree oven to recrisp the duck. Glaze the duck with the sauce, and cook it for about 7 to 10 minutes. Serve the crispy glazed duck with the remaining sauce.

ROASTED CHICKEN WITH VEGETABLES

Prep time: **10 minutes** | Cook time: **none** | Serves **4**

- One 3-pound free-range chicken, giblets removed
- Kosher salt and freshly ground black pepper
- 1 cup coarsely chopped onions (about 1 medium-size onion)
- Four 5-inch sprigs fresh rosemary
- Four 5-inch sprigs fresh thyme
- 1/2 cup plus 1 tablespoon olive oil
- 2 large carrots, peeled and cut into 2-inch pieces
- 3 medium-size red or Yukon Gold potatoes, peeled and quartered
- 3 cloves garlic
- 1/2 cup dry white wine

1. Preheat the oven to 350° F.
2. Rinse the chicken and pat it dry. Salt and pepper the inside of the cavity, and fill it with half the chopped onions, 2 sprigs of the rosemary, and 2 sprigs of the thyme. Truss the chicken and rub all over with 1 tablespoon of the olive oil. Place in a roasting pan or a large baking dish.
3. In a bowl, toss the remaining 2 sprigs each rosemary and thyme, the remaining onions and the carrots, potatoes, garlic, and 1/2 cup olive oil. Season with salt and pepper. Surround the chicken with the vegetables. Pour the wine over the vegetables and bake, stirring the vegetables occasionally, until the chicken juices run clear and the vegetables are roasted, about 11/4 hours.
4. Remove the chicken from the oven and transfer it to a cutting board. Allow to rest for 5 minutes before carving and arranging on a platter. Remove the vegetables from the roasting pan with a slotted spoon and arrange around the chicken. Serve immediately with the pan juices.

DUCK ROASTED WITH SAUERKRAUT

Prep time: **10 minutes** | Cook time: **1 hour 42 minutes** | Serves **4**

- 5 fresh bay leaves
- 1 sprig fresh rosemary
- 10 black peppercorns
- 4-pound duck
- ¼ teaspoon kosher salt
- Freshly ground black pepper
- ½ cup vegetable oil, for browning
- 2 tablespoons extra-virgin olive oil
- 5 garlic cloves, crushed and peeled
- 3 pounds sauerkraut, rinsed well and drained
- 2 cups Chicken Stock

1. Preheat the oven to 475 degrees. Lay the bay leaves, rosemary, and peppercorns on a piece of cheesecloth, and tie with kitchen twine into a sachet. Season the duck all over with the salt and some pepper. Heat a large straight-sided skillet over medium heat and add the vegetable oil. Brown the duck well on all sides, about 10 minutes in all. Remove the duck, pour out any excess oil and put the duck back, breast side up. Roast in the oven until it is very brown and much of the fat is rendered, about 30 minutes.

2. Heat a large Dutch oven, big enough to hold the duck and the sauerkraut, over medium heat. Add the olive oil. Add the garlic, and cook until it is golden, about 2 minutes. Add the sauerkraut, and toss to coat it in the oil. Pour in 2 cups chicken stock, and nestle the herb sachet in the sauerkraut. Put the duck on top of the sauerkraut. Pour the juices from the duck skillet into a spouted measuring cup (or a defatting cup, if you have one), and spoon off as much fat as possible. Pour the defatted juices into the sauerkraut, and bring the liquid to a simmer. With the lid ajar, simmer until the duck is tender, about 1 hour.

3. Discard the herb sachet and remove the duck to a cutting board, and let it rest 5 minutes. Carve into eight serving pieces, and serve with the sauerkraut.

LUSCIOUS TOMATO CHICKEN

Prep time: **10 minutes** | Cook time: **80 minutes** | Serves **4**

- 3 tbsp olive oil
- 1 (32-oz) can diced tomatoes
- 4 chicken breast halves
- 2 whole cloves
- ¼ cup chicken broth
- 2 tbsp tomato paste
- ¼ tsp chili flakes
- 1 tsp ground allspice
- ½ tsp dried mint
- 1 cinnamon stick
- Salt and black pepper to taste

1. Place the tomatoes, chicken broth, olive oil, tomato paste, chili flakes, mint, allspice, cloves, cinnamon stick, salt, and pepper in a pot over medium heat and bring just to a boil.

2. Then, lower the heat and simmer for 30 minutes.

3. Strain the sauce through a fine-mesh sieve and discard the cloves and cinnamon stick.

4. Let it cool completely.

5. Preheat oven to 350 F.

6. Lay the chicken on a baking dish and pour the sauce over.

7. Bake covered with aluminum foil for 40-45 minutes.

8. Uncover and continue baking for 5 more minutes.

9. Serve and enjoy!

CLASSIC TURKEY STEW

Prep time: 10 minutes | Cook time: 51 minutes | Serves 4

- 1 skinless, boneless turkey breast, cubed
- 2 tbsp olive oil
- Salt and black pepper to taste
- 1 tbsp sweet paprika
- ½ cup chicken stock
- 1 lb pearl onions
- 2 garlic cloves, minced
- 1 carrot, sliced
- 1 tsp cumin, ground
- 1 tbsp basil, chopped
- 1 tbsp cilantro, chopped

1. Warm olive oil in a pot over medium heat and sear turkey for 8 minutes, stirring occasionally.
2. Stir in pearl onions, carrot, and garlic and cook for another 3 minutes.
3. Season with salt, pepper, cumin, and paprika.
4. Pour in the stock and bring to a boil; cook for 40 minutes.
5. Top with basil and cilantro.

SICILIAN-STYLE CHICKEN

Prep time: 10 minutes | Cook time: 25 minutes | Serves 4

- 3 tablespoons olive oil
- 1 garlic clove, minced
- Red pepper flakes
- 1½ pounds chicken tenders
- 1 pint cherry tomatoes, halved
- 1 cup olives, pitted and halved
- 3 tablespoons capers, rinsed if desired
- Salt
- 1 cup dry white wine
- 1 cup water

1. In a large sauté pan over medium heat, combine the oil, garlic, and red pepper flakes. Heat for 1 minute while stirring gently with a wooden spoon so the garlic does not burn.
2. Add the chicken and brown on all sides. Add the cherry tomatoes, olives, capers, and salt to taste.
3. Add the wine and let it evaporate, then add the water, reduce the heat to low, cover, and cook for 20 minutes until the tenders are fully cooked.

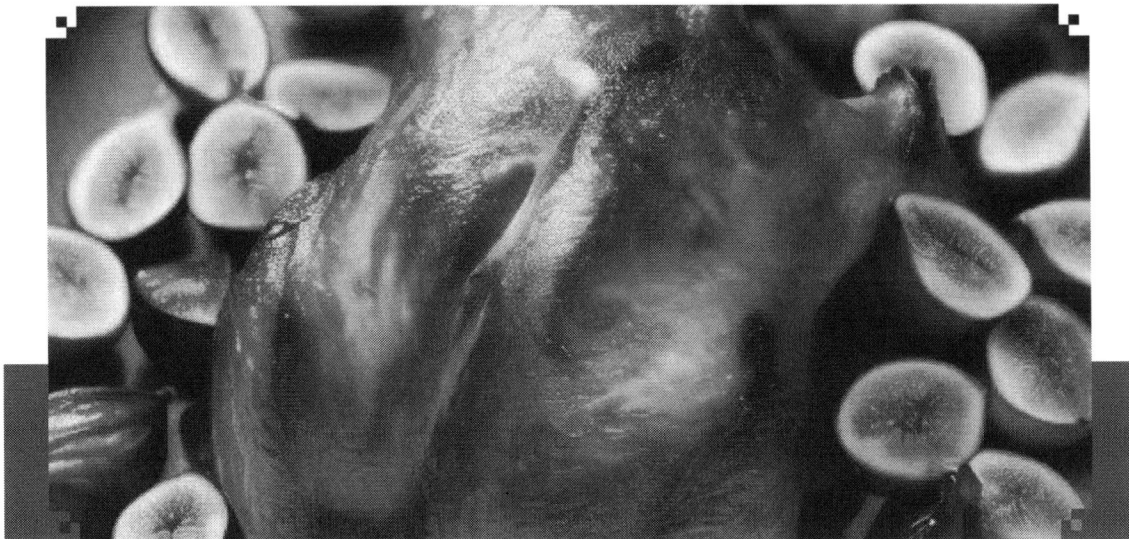

ROAST DUCK WITH FRESH FIGS

Prep time: 10 minutes | Cook time: 1 hour 43 minutes | Serves 4

- One 4-pound duck
- Two 5-inch sprigs fresh rosemary
- 6 fresh sage leaves
- 4 cloves garlic, crushed
- 1/2 medium-size onion
- 2 tablespoons olive oil
- Kosher salt and freshly ground black pepper
- 1/2 cup coarsely chopped onions
- 1/2 cup coarsely chopped carrots
- 1/2 cup coarsely chopped celery
- 3 cloves garlic, cut in half
- One 5-inch sprig fresh thyme
- 1/3 cup honey
- 1 tablespoon butter
- 6 large fresh figs, quartered
- 1 cup port

1. Preheat the oven to 400° F.
2. Wash the duck inside and out, reserving the giblets. Pat dry. If there is a long flap of neck skin, cut it off and discard it. Cut the wing tips at the joints and place in a large roasting pan along with the giblets. Set aside. Fill the duck cavity with one of the rosemary sprigs, the sage, and the garlic. Add the onion half, positioning it so that it holds the herbs inside the duck.
3. Warm the olive oil in a large sauté pan set over medium-high heat. Add the duck and sear it, browning it evenly on all sides, 6 to 8 minutes. Remove from the pan and season all over with salt and pepper. Place the duck, breast side down, in the roasting pan. Roast, turning once, to render the fat, about 30 minutes.
4. Add the chopped onions, carrots, celery, and halved garlic to the roasting pan, distributing them evenly around the duck. Cook to soften the vegetables, about 15 minutes. Add the remaining rosemary sprig and the thyme sprig. Continue cooking to begin to brown the vegetables, about 15 minutes.
5. Reduce the oven to 350° F. Brush one third of the honey over the duck. Continue roasting until the duck is golden brown and cooked through, about 30 minutes. During this time, brush the duck twice with additional honey and stir the vegetables.
6. Remove the duck from the oven. Place it on a cutting board and cover with aluminum foil. Set aside.
7. Remove the giblets and wing tips from the vegetables and discard. Discard the sprigs of herbs. Drain off the fat, reserving about 1/2 cup of the cooking juices. Place the reserved cooking juices and the vegetables in a blender, puree until smooth, and set aside.
8. Melt the butter in a sauté pan set over medium-high heat. Stir in the figs and cook until softened and lightly browned, about 5 minutes. Pour in the port. Allow to simmer until reduced by half, about 8 minutes. Stir in the pureed vegetables and simmer gently to warm through, about 2 minutes. Cut the duck into portions and serve, topping each portion with some of the sauce.

TURKEY VEGETABLE TRAYBAKE

Prep time: **10 minutes** | Cook time: **50 minutes** | Serves **4**

- 2 tbsp olive oil
- 1 lb turkey breast, cubed
- 1 head broccoli, cut into florets
- 2 oz cherry tomatoes, halved
- 2 tbsp cilantro, chopped
- 1 lemon, zested
- Salt and black pepper to taste
- 2 spring onions, chopped

1. Preheat oven to 360 F.
2. Warm the olive oil in a skillet over medium heat and sauté spring onions and lemon zest for 3 minutes.
3. Add in turkey and cook for another 5-6 minutes, stirring occasionally.
4. Transfer to a baking dish, pour in 1 cup of water and bake for 30 minutes.
5. Add in broccoli and tomatoes and bake for another 10 minutes.
6. Top with cilantro.

PISTACHIO TURKEY BREASTS

Prep time: **10 minutes** | Cook time: **40 minutes** | Serves **4**

- ½ cup toasted pistachios, chopped
- 1 tbsp olive oil
- 1 lb turkey breast, cubed
- 1 cup chicken stock
- 1 tbsp basil, chopped
- 1 tbsp rosemary, chopped
- 1 tbsp oregano, chopped
- 1 tbsp parsley, chopped
- 1 tbsp tarragon, chopped
- 3 garlic cloves, minced
- 3 cups tomatoes, chopped

1. Warm olive oil in a skillet over medium heat and cook turkey and garlic for 5 minutes.
2. Stir in stock, basil, rosemary, oregano, parsley, tarragon, pistachios, and tomatoes and bring to a simmer.
3. Cook for 35 minutes.
4. Serve immediately.

BRAISED DUCK LEGS

Prep time: **5 minutes** | Cook time: **90 minutes** | Serves **4**

- 2 tablespoons olive oil
- 3 garlic cloves, crushed
- 3 bay leaves
- 12 black olives, pitted and chopped
- 1 rosemary sprig
- 4 whole duck legs, trimmed of excess fat
- Salt
- Freshly ground black pepper
- 2 cups white wine

1. In a large pot or Dutch oven, heat the oil with the garlic, bay leaves, olives, and rosemary, and sauté for 1 minute over medium heat.
2. Add the duck legs and sauté for a few minutes on each side until brown. Salt and pepper to taste. Add the white wine and bring to a boil.
3. Cover the pan and cook for about 1 hour and 15 minutes (or longer for bigger legs). Check and turn the legs over every 20 to 30 minutes. You should have plenty of liquid when cooking duck from all the fat in the skin, so don't worry about the meat sticking to the bottom of the pan. Check with a fork for doneness before serving.

PEPPERY CHICKEN SAUSAGES

Prep time: **10 minutes** | Cook time: **15 minutes** | Serves **4**

- 2 tbsp olive oil
- 4 chicken sausage links
- 2 garlic cloves, minced
- 1 onion, thinly sliced
- 1 red bell pepper, sliced
- 1 green bell pepper, sliced
- ½ cup dry white wine
- Salt and black pepper to taste
- ½ dried chili pepper, minced

1. Warm olive oil in a pan over medium heat and brown the sausages for 6 minutes, turning periodically.
2. Set aside.
3. In the same pan, sauté onion and bell peppers and garlic for 5 minutes until tender.
4. Deglaze with the wine and stir in salt, pepper, and chili.
5. Simmer for 4 minutes until the sauce reduces by half.
6. Serve sausages topped with bell peppers.

BRAISED DUCK LEGS

Prep time: **5 minutes** | Cook time: **90 minutes** | Serves **4**

- 2 tablespoons olive oil
- 3 garlic cloves, crushed
- 3 bay leaves
- 12 black olives, pitted and chopped
- 1 rosemary sprig
- 4 whole duck legs, trimmed of excess fat
- Salt
- Freshly ground black pepper
- 2 cups white wine

1. In a large pot or Dutch oven, heat the oil with the garlic, bay leaves, olives, and rosemary, and sauté for 1 minute over medium heat.
2. Add the duck legs and sauté for a few minutes on each side until brown. Salt and pepper to taste. Add the white wine and bring to a boil.
3. Cover the pan and cook for about 1 hour and 15 minutes (or longer for bigger legs). Check and turn the legs over every 20 to 30 minutes. You should have plenty of liquid when cooking duck from all the fat in the skin, so don't worry about the meat sticking to the bottom of the pan. Check with a fork for doneness before serving.

CHAPTER 8: PORK, BEEF AND LAMB

CHEESE & SPINACH STUFFED PORK LOIN

Prep time: **10 minutes** | Cook time: **55 minutes** | Serves **6**

- 1 ½ lb pork tenderloin
- 6 slices pancetta, chopped
- 1 cup mushrooms, sliced
- 5 sundried tomatoes, diced
- Salt and black pepper to taste

1. Place a skillet over medium heat and stir-fry the pancetta for 5 minutes until crispy.
2. Add the mushrooms and sauté for another 4-5 minutes until tender, stirring occasionally.
3. Stir in sundried tomatoes and season with salt and pepper; set aside.
4. Preheat the oven to 350F.
5. Using a sharp knife, cut the pork tenderloin in half lengthwise, leaving about 1-inch border; be careful not to cut through to the other side.
6. Open the tenderloin like a book to form a large rectangle.
7. Flatten it to about ¼-inch thickness with a meat tenderizer.
8. Season the pork generously with salt and pepper.
9. Top all over with pancetta filling.
10. Roll up pork tenderloin and tightly secure with kitchen twine.
11. Place on a greased baking sheet.
12. Bake for 60-75 minutes until the pork is cooked through, depending on the thickness of the pork.
13. Remove from the oven and let rest for 10 minutes at room temperature.
14. Remove the twine and discard.
15. Slice the pork into medallions and serve.

SAUERKRAUT WITH PORK

Prep time: **10 minutes** | Cook time: **1 hour 40 minutes** | Serves **6 to 8**

- 1 pound smoked pork butt, halved
- 1 pound kielbasa
- 1 pound smoked pork ribs
- 2 tablespoons extra-virgin olive oil
- 4 pounds sauerkraut, rinsed well and drained
- 2 garlic cloves, thinly sliced
- 6 fresh bay leaves
- Kosher salt
- Freshly ground black pepper
- Fresh horseradish (optional)

1. Put the pork butt, kielbasa, and ribs in a large Dutch oven with water to cover. Bring to a boil. Simmer 10 minutes, drain, reserve the meat, and clean out the pot.
2. To the Dutch oven, off the heat, add the olive oil. Add a layer of half of the sauerkraut. Sprinkle the garlic and bay leaves over the sauerkraut. Arrange the reserved meat over the seasonings. Cover it with the remaining sauerkraut. Pour in 2 cups water. Bring to a boil, reduce the heat to keep it at a simmer, and cover; cook, occasionally stirring from the bottom up, until the ribs are tender, about 45 minutes.
3. Remove the ribs and kielbasa and keep them warm in a low oven. Simmer the sauerkraut, stirring occasionally, until the rest of the pork is tender and the liquid in the pot is almost reduced away, about 20 to 30 minutes more. Remove the bay leaves and garlic, and season with salt and pepper.
4. Return the ribs and kielbasa to the pot, cover, and let sit off the heat 15 minutes. Slice the meats and arrange them on a serving platter, with the sauerkraut at center. Grate some fresh horseradish over the sliced meats, if desired.

MUSTARDY PORK TENDERLOIN

Prep time: **10 minutes** | Cook time: **30 minutes** | Serves **4**

- 2 tbsp olive oil
- 1 (1 ½-oz) pork tenderloin
- 2 garlic cloves, minced
- ½ cup fresh parsley, chopped
- 1 tbsp rosemary, chopped
- 1 tbsp tarragon, chopped
- 3 tbsp stone-ground mustard
- ½ tsp cumin powder
- ½ chili pepper, minced
- Salt and black pepper to taste

1. Preheat your oven to 400 F.
2. In a food processor, blend parsley, tarragon, rosemary, mustard, olive oil, chili pepper, cumin, salt, garlic, and pepper until smooth.
3. Rub the mixture all over the pork and transfer onto a lined baking sheet.
4. Bake in the oven for 20-25 minutes.
5. Slice and serve.

RUSTIC SAUSAGE MEATBALLS

Prep time: **15 minutes** | Cook time: **20 minutes** | Serves **4 to 6**

- 1½ pounds Italian sausage meat, or 5 or 6 Italian sausages, casings removed
- ¼ cup fresh Italian parsley leaves, minced
- Salt
- Freshly ground black pepper

1. Preheat the oven to 375°F.
2. Place the sausage meat and parsley in a medium mixing bowl. Season lightly with salt and pepper. with a large spoon, or your hands, mix until well combined.
3. Line a sheet pan with foil. Make 1-inch or 2-inch balls of meat mixture and line them up on the sheet pan.
4. Roast for about 20 minutes until cooked through and golden.

STUFFED PEPPERS WITH BEEF

Prep time: **10 minutes** | Cook time: **50 minutes** | Serves **4**

- 2 tbsp olive oil
- 2 red bell peppers
- 1 lb ground beef
- 1 shallot, finely chopped
- 2 garlic cloves, minced
- 2 tbsp fresh sage, chopped
- Salt and black pepper to taste
- 1 tsp ground allspice
- ½ cup fresh parsley, chopped
- ½ cup baby arugula leaves
- ½ cup pine nuts, chopped
- 1 tbsp orange juice

1. Warm the olive oil in a large skillet over medium heat.
2. Sauté the beef, garlic, and shallot for 8-10 minutes until the meat is browned and cooked through.
3. Season with sage, allspice, salt, and pepper and remove from the heat to cool slightly.
4. Stir in parsley, arugula, pine nuts, and orange juice and mix.
5. Preheat oven to 390 F.
6. Slice the peppers in half lengthwise and remove the seeds and membranes.
7. Spoon the filling into the pepper halves.
8. Bake in the oven for 25-30 minutes.

BALSAMIC VINEGAR STEAK

Prep time: **5 minutes** | Cook time: **8 minutes** | Serves **4**

- ½ cup balsamic vinegar
- ¼ cup olive oil, plus 1 tablespoon, divided
- 1 teaspoon chopped fresh parsley
- 2 garlic cloves, minced
- 4 (5-ounce) boneless rib eye steaks, such as Delmonico
- Salt
- Freshly ground black pepper

1. In a small bowl, mix the balsamic vinegar, ¼ cup of oil, parsley, and garlic. Brush the steaks with the marinade, and season with salt and pepper.
2. In a large skillet over medium heat, heat the remaining 1 tablespoon of olive oil. When the oil is hot, add the steaks to the pan, reserving the remaining marinade. Cook the steaks to your desired doneness, 3 to 4 minutes per side for medium-rare.
3. Once cooked, remove the steaks from the pan and place them on a plate, covering them with aluminum foil.
4. Add the leftover marinade to the hot pan, cook for 2 to 3 minutes until the marinade is reduced by half. Uncover the steaks and pour the reduced glaze on top.

FRUITY PORK CHOPS

Prep time: **10 minutes** | Cook time: **30 minutes** | Serves **4**

- 2 tbsp olive oil
- ½ tsp cayenne powder
- 4 pork chops, boneless
- ¼ cup peach preserves
- 1 tbsp thyme, chopped

1. In a large bowl, mix peach preserves, olive oil, and cayenne powder.
2. Preheat your grill to medium.
3. Rub pork chops with some peach glaze and grill for 10 minutes.
4. Turn the chops, rub more glaze and cook for 10 minutes.
5. Top with thyme.

FILET MIGNON IN MUSHROOM SAUCE

Prep time: **10 minutes** | Cook time: **25 minutes** | Serves **2**

- 8 oz cremini mushrooms, quartered
- 2 tbsp olive oil
- 2 filet mignon steaks
- 1 shallot, minced
- 2 tsp flour
- 2 tsp tomato paste
- ½ cup red wine
- 1 cup chicken stock
- ½ tsp dried thyme
- 1 fresh rosemary sprig
- 1 tsp herbes de Provence
- Salt and black pepper to taste
- ¼ tsp garlic powder
- ¼ tsp shallot powder
- ¼ tsp mustard powder

1. Warm 1 tbsp of olive oil in a saucepan over medium heat. Add the mushrooms and shallot and stir-fry for 5-8 minutes. Stir in the flour and tomato paste and cook for another 30 seconds. Pour in the wine and scrape up any browned bits from the sauté pan.

2. Add the chicken stock, thyme, and rosemary. Bring it to a boil and cook until the sauce thickens, 2-4 minutes. In a small bowl, mix the herbes de Provence, salt, garlic powder, shallot powder, mustard powder, salt, and pepper. Rub the beef with the herb mixture on both sides.

3. Warm the remaining olive oil in a sauté over medium heat. Sear the beef for 2-3 minutes on each side. Serve topped with mushroom sauce.

GRILLED BUTTERFLIED LEG OF LAMB

Prep time: **10 minutes** | Cook time: **30 minutes** | Serves **6 to 8**

- 1 boneless butterflied leg of lamb (about 4 pounds off the bone)
- ¼ cup olive oil
- 2 cloves garlic, crushed
- 2 fresh sage leaves
- Two 5-inch sprigs fresh rosemary, cut in half
- Two 5-inch sprigs fresh oregano, torn into pieces, or ¼ teaspoon dried
- ½ cup dry red wine
- 1 medium-size onion, cut into 1-inch-thick slices
- 1 tablespoon balsamic vinegar
- ½ lemon, quartered

1. Place the lamb in a large glass baking dish or sealable plastic bag. In a medium-size bowl, mix the olive oil, garlic, sage, rosemary, oregano, wine, onion, and vinegar. Add the lemon sections, squeezing them gently to release some of the juice. Pour this over the lamb, cover, and refrigerate for at least 2 hours, basting the meat occasionally. Allow the meat to return to room temperature before grilling.

2. Prepare a grill that has a cover. Cook the meat on the grill, covered, basting once or twice with the marinade, until well browned on one side, about 12 minutes. Turn the meat over and baste once. Cover the grill and cook the meat for 12 minutes more for medium to medium-rare, and 15 minutes for medium-well to well-done meat. (Rare lamb registers 160° F on a meat thermometer; well done is 175° F. If the fire flares around the meat, remove the cover and spray the fire with water to prevent charring.) Remove from the grill, cover with a sheet of aluminum foil, and allow to rest for 5 to 10 minutes before carving.

GARLICKY PORK CHOPS

Prep time: **10 minutes** | Cook time: **45 minutes** | Serves **4**

- 1 tbsp olive oil
- 4 pork loin chops, boneless
- Salt and black pepper to taste
- 4 garlic cloves, minced
- 1 tbsp thyme, chopped

1. Preheat oven to 390 F.
2. Place pork chops, salt, pepper, garlic, thyme, and olive oil in a roasting pan and bake for 10 minutes.
3. Decrease the heat to 360 F and bake for 25 minutes.

ROASTED BEEF WITH KALE SLAW & BELL PEPPERS

Prep time: **10 minutes** | Cook time: **35 minutes** | Serves **4**

- 2 tsp olive oil
- 1 lb skirt steak
- 4 cups kale slaw
- 1 tbsp garlic powder
- Salt and black pepper to taste
- 1 small red onion, sliced
- 10 sundried tomatoes, halved
- ½ red bell pepper, sliced

1. Preheat your broiler.
2. Brush steak with olive oil, salt, garlic powder, and pepper and place under the broiler for 10 minutes, turning once.
3. Remove to a cutting board and let rest for 10 minutes, then cut the steak diagonally.
4. In the meantime, place sun-dried tomatoes, kale slaw, onion, and bell pepper in a bowl and mix to combine.
5. Transfer to a serving plate and top with steak slices to serve.

SPICE-RUBBED PORK TENDERLOIN

Prep time: **8 minutes** | Cook time: **35 minutes** | Serves **4 to 6**

- 2 teaspoons sweet paprika
- 2 teaspoons crushed red pepper or 1 teaspoon cayenne
- 2 teaspoons ground cumin
- 1 teaspoon ground fennel or fennel pollen
- Salt
- 2 pork tenderloins, about 1 pound each
- 2–3 tablespoons extra-virgin olive oil, and more for drizzling
- 2 medium onions, peeled and quartered

1. Preheat the oven 375°F.
2. In a small mixing bowl mix together the paprika, crushed red pepper, cumin, fennel, and a few healthy shakes of salt. Rub the spice mix all over the meat.
3. Heat tablespoons olive oil in an ovenproof casserole or skillet with at least 2-inch sides. Sear and brown the pork on all sides, about 5 minutes.
4. Scatter onions around the pork. Transfer the casserole uncovered to the oven. Roast for about 30 minutes, until an instant-read thermometer reads 145.
5. Take pork out, tent with some foil, and let rest for about 10 minutes before cutting. There will be some "carry-over" cooking as the meat rests. Cut into thin slices, serve with the onions and juices.

PORK WITH OLIVES

Prep time: **10 minutes** | Cook time: **25 minutes** | Serves **4**

- 1 small pork tenderloin, cut into 1½-inch-thick rounds
- ½ cup flour
- Salt
- Freshly ground black pepper
- ¼ cup olive oil
- 3 sprigs rosemary, leaves only, stemmed
- 1 cup dry white wine
- ½ cup green olives, pitted and halved

1. Gently coat the pork tenderloin pieces in the flour. Season with salt and pepper. Set aside.
2. In a large sauté pan over medium-high heat, heat the oil and rosemary for a few minutes.
3. Add the pork to the oil and brown on all sides. Add the white wine and olives.
4. Reduce the heat to low, and continue cooking the pork for an additional 15 to 20 minutes, uncovered. If the juices are drying up too quickly, reduce the heat and add a little bit of water. A little bit of juice should remain to top the meat with before serving.

OVEN-BAKED PORK CHOPS

Prep time: **10 minutes** | Cook time: **20 to 25 minutes** | Serves **4**

- Nonstick cooking spray
- 1 cup bread crumbs
- ½ cup grated Parmesan cheese
- 4 bone-in pork chops
- Salt
- Freshly ground black pepper
- 2 eggs, lightly beaten
- Olive oil, for drizzling

1. Preheat the oven to 375°F. Spray a baking sheet with cooking spray and set aside.
2. In a medium bowl, stir together the bread crumbs and cheese.
3. Sprinkle the pork chops with salt and pepper, and dip them in the beaten eggs. Coat the chops in the bread crumb and cheese mixture and gently place them on the prepared baking sheet. Add a light drizzle of oil.
4. Bake for 20 to 25 minutes, depending on the thickness of the chops. Gently, so as not to remove any of the outer coating, turn the chops over once midway through baking.

ONE-PAN SAUSAGE AND PEPPERS

Prep time: **15 minutes** | Cook time: **40 minutes** | Serves **4 to 6**

- 2 medium onions
- 3 red or green bell peppers, or a mixture
- 6 to 8 Italian sausages
- Extra-virgin olive oil, for drizzling
- Salt
- Freshly ground black pepper

1. Preheat the oven to 400°F.
2. Peel the onions and cut them into ½-inch wedges. Cut the peppers in half. Pull out the stem and seeds. Cut the peppers into ½-inch strips.
3. Using kitchen scissors, cut each sausage into 3 or 4 pieces (you can use a knife, but scissors are easier with raw sausages).
4. Line a sheet pan with foil. Drizzle some olive oil to lightly coat. Sprinkle cut onions and peppers over the pan. Scatter the sausage pieces. Drizzle a little olive oil over everything. Season with salt and pepper to taste.
5. Roast in the oven for about 40 minutes until vegetables and sausage are cooked through and starting to brown. Turn vegetables and sausages 1 to 2 times while cooking.
6. Serve hot or warm on a large platter.

PRUNE-STUFFED ROAST LOIN OF PORK

Prep time: **10 minutes** | Cook time: **1 hour 10 minutes** | Serves **8**

- 8 ounces dried pitted prunes
- ½ cup bourbon
- 3-pound boneless center pork loin roast, trimmed
- 10 fresh sage leaves
- Kosher salt
- Freshly ground black pepper

- 2 tablespoons extra-virgin olive oil
- ½ cup finely diced carrot
- ½ cup finely diced celery
- ½ cup roughly chopped onion
- 4 garlic cloves, crushed and peeled
- 2½ cups Chicken Stock

1. In a small bowl, soak the prunes in bourbon 1 hour. Preheat the oven to 450 degrees. Drain the prunes, and set four of them aside along with the soaking liquid.
2. To stuff the roast: Use a sharp knife to cut a 1-inch pocket along the entire length of the eye, around the top half of the roast, like forming a tunnel. Cut from both sides of the roast until you cut through.
3. Stuff three quarters of the soaked prunes into the slit in the roast, and tie the roast securely with kitchen twine at 2-inch intervals. Thread the sage leaves underneath the ties on either side of the roast. Season the roast generously with salt and pepper, and rub it with the olive oil.
4. Put the roast in a large roasting pan, and roast 15 minutes. Reduce the oven temperature to 400 degrees. Tilt the roasting pan, and spoon off excess fat. Scatter the carrot, celery, onion, and garlic around the roast. Roast an additional 15 minutes. Add the reserved prunes and soaking liquid, and roast 10 minutes. Pour the stock into the pan, and continue cooking, basting the roast occasionally with the pan juices, until a meat thermometer inserted into the thickest part of the roast registers 145 degrees, about 30 minutes more.
5. Remove the roast to a platter. Pass the contents of the pan through a food mill fitted with the fine disk into a small bowl. (Alternatively, strain the liquid through a sieve, pressing on the vegetables to extract as much liquid as possible and to force some of the vegetables through the sieve.) Skim all fat from the surface of the sauce. The sauce should be thick enough to coat a spoon lightly. If not, transfer it to a small saucepan and reduce a bit more. Season the sauce with salt and pepper, if needed. Cut the meat into ¼-inch slices, and serve it with the sauce.

FRIED MEATBALLS

Prep time: **15 minutes** | Cook time: **20 minutes** | Serves **4**

- 2 slices white bread
- ¼ cup milk
- 3 tablespoons freshly grated Parmesan cheese
- 1 egg

- Salt
- 1 pound ground meat (beef, pork, or veal)
- ½ cup bread crumbs
- Vegetable for frying

1. Remove the crusts from the bread slices and break into small pieces. Add the bread pieces to a bowl and pour in the milk. Let rest for a couple of minutes so that the bread absorbs the milk.
2. with a fork or your fingers, break the bread into tiny pieces. Add the Parmesan cheese, egg, salt, and ground meat. Mix with a fork, or your hand, keeping the mixture soft.
3. Spoon out some of the mixture at a time and roll it between the palms of your hands, without pressing too hard. Make meatballs about the size of golf balls.
4. In a sauté pan or skillet, pour enough oil to cover the bottom of the skillet and heat the oil over medium-high heat. Roll the meatballs in the bread crumbs and cook for 3 minutes on each side, turning only when golden. Lower the heat to medium and cook for another 5 to 10 minutes, depending on size, turning occasionally, until fully cooked. Drain on a paper towel, and serve hot or warm.

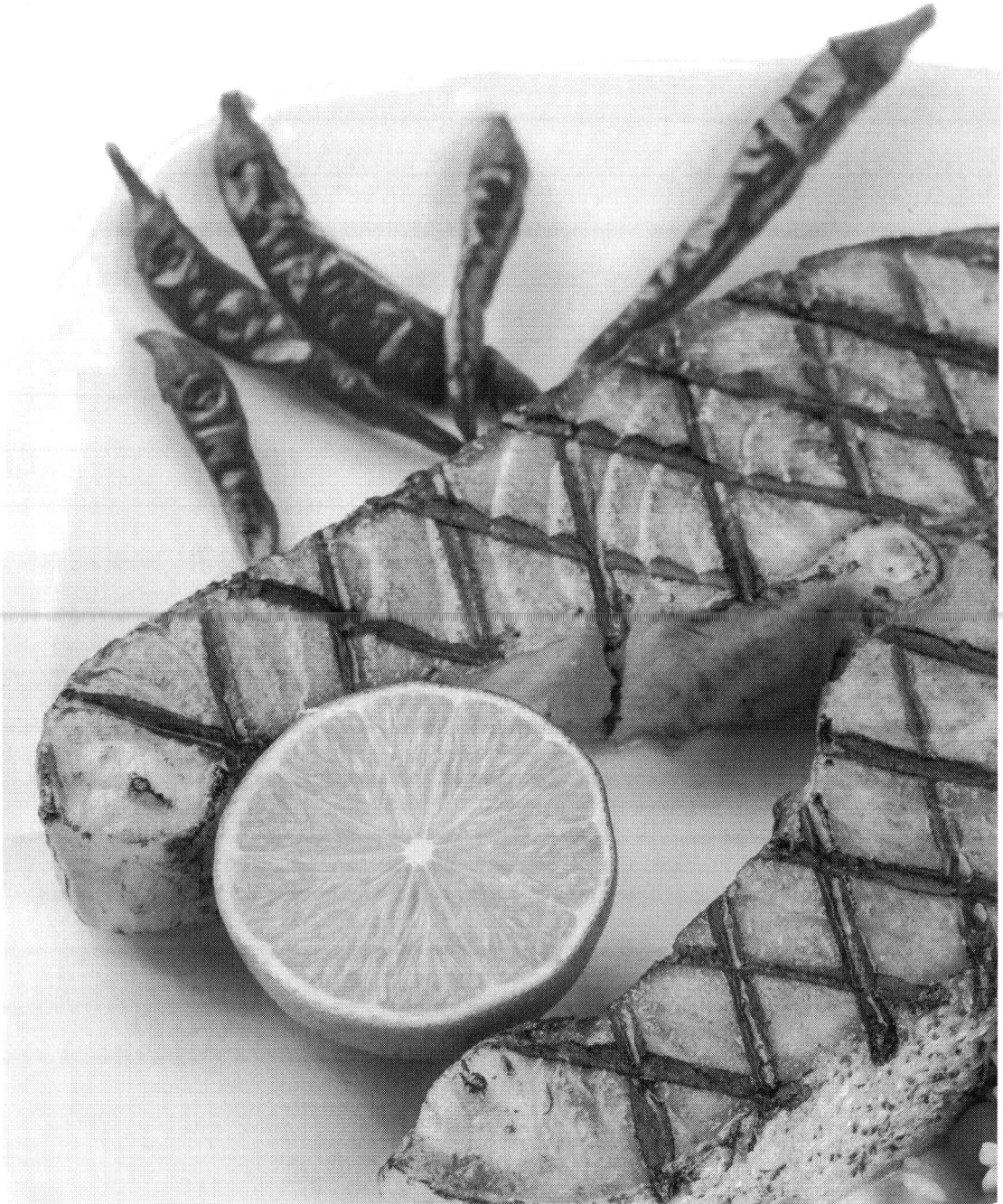

CHAPTER 9: FISH AND SEAFOOD

FRIED CALAMARI

Prep time: **10 minutes** | Cook time: **25 minutes** | Serves **4**

- 2½ pounds whole squid or 2 pounds cleaned squid, sliced into rings
- vegetable oil for frying
- 1 cup flour, spread on a plate
- a spatter screen
- salt

1. If cleaning the squid yourself, follow the directions on to . Slice the sac into rings a little less than ½ inch wide, and separate the cluster of tentacles into two parts. Whether cleaning it yourself or using it already cleaned, wash all parts in cold water and pat thoroughly dry with cloth or paper towels.
2. Pour enough oil into a frying pan to come 1½ inches up the sides, and turn on the heat to high.
3. When the oil is very hot—test it with 1 calamari ring, if it sizzles it's ready—put the rings and tentacles into a large strainer, pour flour over them, shake off the excess flour, grab a handful of squid at a time, and slip it into the pan. Do not crowd the pan; fry the calamari in two or more batches, depending on the size of the pan. Squid may burst while frying, spraying hot oil. Hold the spatter screen over the pan to protect yourself.
4. The moment the calamari is done to a tawny gold on one side, turn it and do the other side. When done, use a slotted spoon or spatula to transfer it to a cooling rack to drain or spread on a platter lined with paper towels. When all the calamari is cooked and out of the pan, sprinkle with salt and serve at once while still piping hot.

TOMATO & SQUID STEW

Prep time: **10 minutes** | Cook time: **50 minutes** | Serves **4**

- 1 (28-oz) cans whole peeled tomatoes, diced
- ¼ cup olive oil
- 1 onion, chopped
- 1 celery rib, sliced
- 3 garlic cloves, minced
- ¼ tsp red pepper flakes
- 1 red chili, minced
- ½ cup dry white wine
- 2 lb squid, sliced into rings
- Salt and black pepper to taste
- ⅓ cup green olives, chopped
- 1 tbsp capers
- 2 tbsp fresh parsley, chopped

1. Warm olive oil in a pot over medium heat.
2. Sauté the onion, garlic, red chili, and celery until softened, about 5 minutes.
3. Stir in pepper flakes and cook for about 30 seconds.
4. Stir in wine, scraping up any browned bits, and cook until nearly evaporated, about 1 minute.
5. Add 1 cup of water and season with salt and pepper.
6. Stir the squid in the pot.
7. Reduce heat to low, cover, and simmer until squid has released its liquid, about 15 minutes.
8. Pour in tomatoes, olives, and capers, and continue to cook until squid is very tender, 30-35 minutes.
9. Top with parsley.
10. Serve and enjoy!

GRILLED TUNA STEAKS

Prep time: **5 minutes** | Cook time: **10 minutes** | Makes **4 main-course**

- 2 ahi tuna steaks (each about 1 pound and 2 inches thick)
- ¼ cup extra-virgin olive oil
- ¾ teaspoon kosher salt
- ¾ teaspoon freshly ground black pepper
- 2 tablespoons fresh lemon juice (from about ½ lemon)
- Basil Pesto

1. Prepare a charcoal or gas grill for medium-high heat or preheat a ridged grill pan over a medium-high flame.
2. Wash and pat the tuna dry with paper towels.
3. Brush both sides of the tuna with the oil and sprinkle with the salt and pepper.
4. Grill the tuna until just seared on the outside but still rare in the center, about 2 minutes per side.
5. If desired, continue cooking the tuna until just cooked through in the center, about 2 minutes longer per side.
6. Using a metal spatula, transfer the tuna to a cutting board and set aside for 5 minutes.
7. Using a large, sharp knife, cut the tuna across the grain and on a bias into ½-inch-thick slices.
8. Arrange the slices on a serving plate.
9. Drizzle with the lemon juice, and serve with the basil pesto.

ALMOND-CRUSTED SALMON

Prep time: **10 minutes** | Cook time: **20 minutes** | Serves **4**

- 1 tbsp olive oil
- ½ tsp lemon zest
- ¼ cup breadcrumbs
- ½ cup toasted almonds, ground
- ½ tsp dried thyme
- Salt and black pepper to taste
- 4 salmon steaks
- 1 lemon, cut into wedges

1. Preheat oven to 350 F.
2. In a shallow dish, combine the lemon zest, breadcrumbs, almonds, thyme, salt, and pepper.
3. Coat the salmon steaks with olive oil and arrange them on a baking sheet.
4. Cover them with the almond mixture, pressing down lightly with your fingers to create a tightly packed crust.
5. Bake for 10-12 minutes or until the almond crust is lightly browned and the fish is cooked through.
6. Serve garnished with lemon wedges.

TROUT BOWLS WITH AVOCADO & FARRO

Prep time: **10 minutes** | Cook time: **40 minutes** | Serves **4**

- 4 tbsp olive oil
- 8 trout fillets, boneless
- 1 cup farro
- Juice of 2 lemons
- Salt and black pepper to taste
- 1 avocado, chopped
- ¼ cup balsamic vinegar
- 1 garlic clove, minced
- ¼ cup parsley, chopped
- ¼ cup mint, chopped
- 2 tbsp yellow mustard

1. Boil salted water in a pot over medium heat and stir in farro.
2. Simmer for 30 minutes and drain.
3. Remove to a bowl and combine with lemon juice, mustard, garlic, salt, pepper, and half olive oil.
4. Set aside.
5. Mash the avocado with a fork in a bowl and mix with vinegar, salt, pepper, parsley, and mint.
6. Warm the remaining oil in a skillet over medium heat and brown trout fillets skin-side down for 10 minutes on both sides.
7. Let cool and cut into pieces.
8. Put over farro and stir in avocado dressing.
9. Serve immediately.

SQUID AND POTATOES, GENOA STYLE

Prep time: **10 minutes** | Cook time: **35 minutes** | Serves **6**

- 3 pounds small to medium whole squid or 2½ pounds cleaned squid, sliced into rings
- 5 tablespoons extra virgin olive oil
- 2 teaspoons chopped garlic
- 1½ tablespoons chopped parsley
- ⅓ cup dry white wine
- 1 cup canned imported Italian plum tomatoes, cut up, with their juice
- ½ teaspoon chopped fresh marjoram or oregano or ¼ teaspoon dried
- 1¼ pounds boiling potatoes
- salt
- black pepper, ground fresh from the mill

1. If cleaning the squid yourself, follow the directions on to . Slice the sac into rings a little less than ½ inch wide, and separate the cluster of tentacles into two parts. Whether cleaning it yourself or using it already cleaned, wash all parts in cold water and pat thoroughly dry with cloth or paper towels.
2. Put the oil, garlic, and parsley in a sauté pan, turn the heat on to high, and cook the garlic until it becomes colored a light nut brown. Put in all the squid. Use a long-handled fork to turn the squid, looking out for any that may pop, spraying drops of hot oil; do not hunch over the pan.
3. When the squid turns a dull, flat white, add the wine, and let it bubble away for about 2 minutes. Add the cut-up tomatoes with their juice, the marjoram or oregano, and stir thoroughly. Cover the pan and adjust the heat to cook at a slow simmer.
4. While the squid is cooking, peel the potatoes and cut them up into irregular pieces about 1½ inches thick. When the squid has cooked for about 45 minutes and is tender, add salt, the potatoes, and several grindings of pepper, stir thoroughly to coat well, and cover the pan again. Cook, always at a slow simmer, until the potatoes are tender, about 20 to 30 minutes. Taste and correct for salt and pepper and serve promptly.

CRISPY POLLOCK FILLETS

Prep time: **10 minutes** | Cook time: **25 minutes** | Serves **4**

- 4 pollock fillets, boneless
- 2 cups potato chips, crushed
- 2 tbsp mayonnaise

1. Preheat oven to 380F.
2. Line a baking sheet with parchment paper.
3. Rub each fillet with mayonnaise and dip them in the potato chips.
4. Place fillets on the sheet and bake for 12 minutes.
5. Serve with salad.

SEAFOOD MEDLEY

Prep time: **10 minutes** | Cook time: **15 minutes** | Serves **4**

- 2 tbsp butter
- ½ lb squid rings
- 1 lb shrimp, peeled, deveined
- Salt and black pepper to taste
- 2 garlic cloves, minced
- 1 tsp rosemary, dried
- 1 red onion, chopped
- 1 cup vegetable stock
- 1 lemon, juiced
- 1 tbsp parsley, chopped

1. Melt the butter in a skillet over medium heat and cook onion and garlic for 4 minutes.
2. Stir in shrimp, salt, pepper, squid rings, rosemary, vegetable stock, and lemon juice and bring to a boil.
3. Simmer for 8 minutes.
4. Put in parsley and serve.

COD WITH POTATOES

Prep time: **15 minutes** | Cook time: **30 minutes** | Serves **4**

- 3 tablespoons olive oil
- 2 or 3 garlic cloves, sliced
- 2 to 3 tablespoons chopped fresh parsley
- 1 teaspoon dried oregano
- 2 cups canned crushed tomatoes
- 3 medium potatoes, peeled and diced
- 2 cups water, divided
- Salt
- 1½ pounds cod loins

1. In a large sauté pan over medium heat, combine the oil, garlic, and parsley. Cook for about 1 minute, just long enough to heat up the oil.
2. Add the oregano and tomatoes and cook for 5 minutes.
3. Add the potatoes and 1 cup of water, and cook for an additional 5 minutes. Add salt to taste.
4. Add the cod loins to the pan with the remaining 1 cup of water. Simmer, uncovered, for 20 minutes, until the broth has thickened. Serve with crusty bread or pasta.

SHRIMP & VEGETABLE ROAST

Prep time: **10 minutes** | Cook time: **22 minutes** | Serves **4**

- 2 lb shrimp, peeled and deveined
- 4 tbsp olive oil
- 2 bell peppers, cut into chunks
- 2 fennel bulbs, cut into wedges
- 2 red onions, cut into wedges
- 4 garlic cloves, unpeeled
- 8 Kalamata olives, halved
- 1 tsp lemon zest, grated
- 2 tsp oregano, dried
- 2 tbsp parsley, chopped
- Salt and black pepper to taste

1. Preheat oven to 390 F.
2. Place bell peppers, garlic, fennel, red onions, and olives in a roasting tray.
3. Add in the lemon zest, oregano, half of the olive oil, salt, and pepper and toss to coat; roast for 15 minutes.
4. Coat the shrimp with the remaining olive oil and pour over the veggies; roast for another 7 minutes.
5. Serve topped with parsley.

BALSAMIC PRAWNS WITH MUSHROOMS

Prep time: **10 minutes** | Cook time: **25 minutes** | Serves **4**

- 1 lb tiger prawns, peeled and deveined
- 3 tbsp olive oil
- 2 green onions, sliced
- ½ lb white mushrooms, sliced
- 2 tbsp balsamic vinegar
- 2 tsp garlic, minced

1. Warm olive oil in a skillet over medium heat and cook green onions and garlic for 2 minutes.
2. Stir in mushrooms and balsamic vinegar and cook for an additional 6 minutes.
3. Put in prawns and cook for 4 minutes.
4. Serve right away.

SHRIMP BUZARA STYLE

Prep time: **10 minutes** | Cook time: **25 minutes** | Serves **4 to 6**

- 2 pounds super colossal shrimp (10 to 12 per pound)
- 1 tablespoon tomato paste
- 1 cup hot light fish stock
- ¼ cup olive oil
- ½ cup finely chopped onion
- 2 cloves garlic, crushed and peeled
- Salt and freshly ground black pepper to taste
- 1 cup dry white wine
- 1 tablespoon breadcrumbs
- 1 tablespoon chopped fresh Italian parsley

1. Using poultry shears or a sharp paring knife, cut through the outer curve of the shrimp shells from end to end, but don't remove the shells. Rinse the shrimp under cold running water, and devein.
2. Dissolve the tomato paste in the hot stock. Heat 2 tablespoons of olive oil in a medium saucepan. Add the onion and garlic, and sauté over moderately high heat until golden. Season with salt and pepper, add the wine, and bring to a boil. Add the stock-and-tomato-paste mixture, reduce the heat, and simmer 20 minutes.
3. Meantime, heat the remaining oil in a large skillet, add the shrimp, and sauté (in two batches) 1 minute on each side. Drain off the oil, return all the shrimp to the skillet, and add the sauce. Cover, and cook over high heat, stirring occasionally, until the shrimp are just cooked through, about 2 or 3 minutes. Sprinkle with breadcrumbs and parsley, mix well, and cook a minute longer, uncovered. Serve immediately.

BELL PEPPER & FENNEL SALMON

Prep time: **10 minutes** | Cook time: **30 minutes** | Serves **4**

- 2 tbsp olive oil
- 4 salmon fillets, boneless
- 1 fennel bulb, sliced
- Salt and black pepper to taste
- ½ tsp chili powder
- 1 yellow bell pepper, diced
- 1 red bell pepper, chopped
- 1 green bell pepper, chopped

1. In a skillet, warm the olive oil over medium heat.
2. Season the salmon with chili powder, salt, and pepper and cook for 6-8 minutes, turning once.
3. Remove to a serving plate.
4. Add fennel and peppers to the skillet and cook for another 10 minutes until tender.
5. Top the salmon with the mixture.

POACHED COD

Prep time: **10 minutes** | Cook time: **20 minutes** | Serves **4**

- 4 cod fillets, skins removed
- 3 cups olive oil
- Salt and black pepper to taste
- 1 lemon, zested and juiced
- 3 fresh thyme sprigs

1. Heat the oil with thyme sprigs in a pot over low heat.
2. Gently add the cod fillets and poach them for about 6 minutes or until the fish is completely opaque.
3. Using a slotted spoon, carefully remove the fish to a plate lined with paper towels.
4. Sprinkle with lemon zest, salt, and pepper.
5. Drizzle with lemon juice and serve immediately.

SWEET AND SOUR SWORDFISH

Prep time: **15 minutes** | Cook time: **15 minutes** | Serves **4**

- 1 cup water
- 2 tablespoons white wine vinegar
- 1 tablespoon sugar
- 3 tablespoons olive oil, divided
- 4 small or medium red onions, thinly sliced
- Salt
- Freshly ground black pepper
- 2 garlic cloves, minced
- 4 swordfish steaks
- 2 teaspoons dried oregano

6. In a small bowl, mix the water, vinegar, and sugar. Set aside.
7. In a sauté pan over medium heat, combine 2 tablespoons of oil and the onions, and sauté them for 2 minutes. Add the water mixture, season with salt and pepper, cover, and cook the onions for 10 to 15 minutes more.
8. In the meantime, in a separate pan over low heat, heat the remaining 1 tablespoon of oil and the garlic and simmer briefly. Add the swordfish, season with salt and pepper, and cook for 5 to 6 minutes per side, or longer if preferred.
9. Plate the swordfish and top each steak with the sweetened onions. Sprinkle with the oregano.

HORSERADISH TROUT FILLETS

Prep time: **10 minutes** | Cook time: **20 minutes** | Serves **4**

- 3 tbsp olive oil
- 2 tbsp horseradish sauce
- 1 onion, sliced
- 2 tsp Italian seasoning
- 4 trout fillets, boneless
- ¼ cup panko breadcrumbs
- ½ cup green olives, chopped
- Salt and black pepper to taste
- 1 lemon, juiced

1. Preheat the oven to 380 F.
2. Line a baking sheet with parchment paper.
3. Sprinkle trout fillets with salt and pepper and dip in breadcrumbs.
4. Arrange them along with the onion on the sheet.
5. Sprinkle with olive oil, Italian seasoning, and lemon juice and bake for 15-18 minutes.
6. Transfer to a serving plate and top with horseradish sauce and olives.
7. Serve.

CELERY STICKS STUFFED WITH CRAB

Prep time: **10 minutes** | Cook time: **10 minutes** | Serves **4**

- 1 cup cream cheese
- 6 oz crab meat
- 1 tsp Mediterranean seasoning
- 2 tbsp apple cider vinegar
- 8 celery sticks, halved
- Salt and black pepper to taste

1. In a large mixing bowl, combine the cream cheese, crab meat, apple cider vinegar, salt, pepper, and Mediterranean seasoning.
2. Divide the crab mixture between the celery sticks.
3. Serve.

FAVORITE PRAWN SCAMPI

Prep time: **10 minutes** | Cook time: **25 minutes** | Serves **4**

- 1 lb prawns, peeled and deveined
- 2 tbsp olive oil
- 1 onion, chopped
- 6 garlic cloves, minced
- 1 lemon, juiced and zested
- ½ cup dry white wine
- Salt and black pepper to taste
- 2 cups fusilli, cooked
- ½ tsp red pepper flakes

1. Warm olive oil in a pan over medium heat and sauté onion and garlic for 3 minutes, stirring often, until fragrant.
2. Stir in prawns and cook for 3-4 minutes.
3. Mix in lemon juice, lemon zest, salt, pepper, wine, and red flakes.
4. Bring to a boil, then decrease the heat, and simmer for 2 minutes until the liquid is reduced by half.
5. Turn the heat off.
6. Stir in pasta and serve.

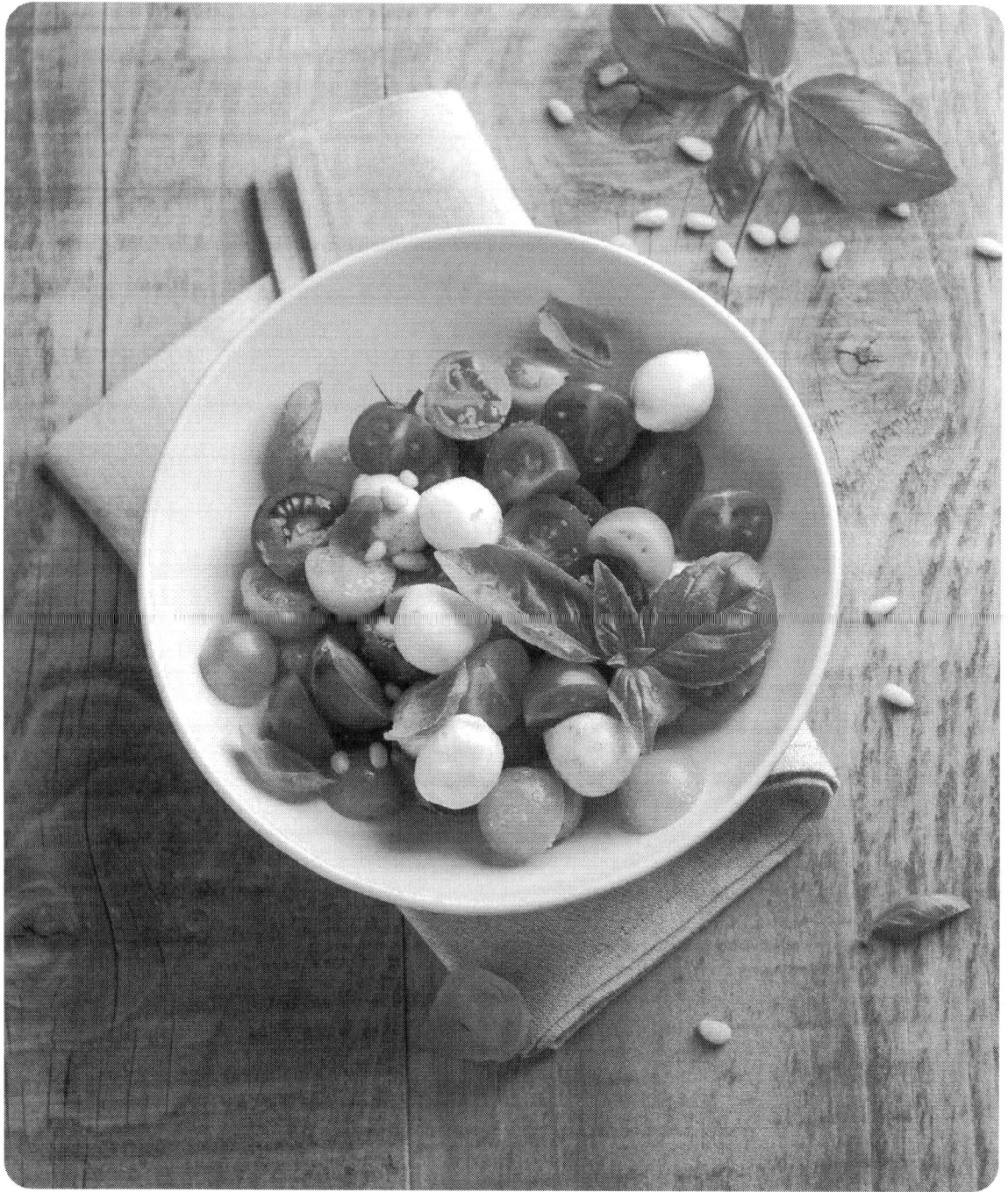

CHAPTER 10: MEATLESS RECIPES

FUSILLI IN CHICKPEA SAUCE

Prep time: **10 minutes** | Cook time: **35 minutes** | Serves **4**

- 1 (15-oz) can chickpeas, drained, liquid reserved
- ¼ cup olive oil
- ½ large shallot, chopped
- 5 garlic cloves, thinly sliced
- 1 cup whole-grain fusilli
- Salt and black pepper to taste
- ¼ cup Parmesan, shaved
- 2 tsp dried parsley
- 1 tsp dried oregano
- A pinch of red pepper flakes

1. Heat olive oil in a skillet over medium heat and sauté the shallot and garlic for 3-5 minutes until the garlic is golden.
2. Add ¾ of the chickpeas and 2 tbsp of the water from the can; bring to a simmer.
3. Remove from the heat, transfer to a blender, and pulse until smooth.
4. Add the remaining chickpeas and some more of the reserved liquid if it's too thick.Bring a large pot of salted water to a boil and cook pasta until al dente, 7-8 minutes.
5. Reserve ½ cup of the pasta liquid, drain the pasta and return it to the pot.
6. Add the chickpea sauce to the hot pasta and keep adding ¼ cup of the pasta liquid until your desired consistency is reached.
7. Place the pasta pot over medium heat and mix occasionally until the sauce thickens.
8. Season with salt and pepper.
9. Sprinkle with freshly grated Parmesan, parsley, oregano, and pepper flakes!

SUNDAY ZITI MARINARA BAKE

Prep time: **10 minutes** | Cook time: **60 minutes** | Serves **4**

- 2 tbsp olive oil
- ¼ onion, diced
- 3 cloves garlic, chopped
- 1 (28-oz) can tomatoes, diced
- Sprig of fresh thyme
- ½ bunch fresh basil
- Salt and pepper to taste
- 1 lb ziti
- 1 cup cottage cheese
- 1 cup grated Mozzarella cheese
- ¾ cup grated Pecorino cheese

1. In a saucepan, warm the olive oil over medium heat.
2. Stir-fry onion and garlic until lightly browned, 3 minutes.
3. Add the tomatoes and herbs and bring to a boil, then simmer for 7 minutes, covered.
4. Set aside.
5. Discard the herb sprigs and stir in salt and pepper to taste.
6. Preheat the oven to 375F.
7. Prepare the pasta according to package directions.
8. Drain and mix the pasta in a bowl along with half of the prepared marinara sauce, cottage cheese, and half the Mozzarella and Pecorino cheeses.
9. Transfer the mixture to a baking dish, and top with the remaining marinara sauce and cheese.
10. Bake for 25 to 35 minutes, or until bubbly and golden brown.
11. Serve warm.

BAKED RED ENDIVE WITH TOMATOES & PANCETTA

Prep time: 10 minutes | Cook time: **45 minutes** | Serves **4**

- 2 tablespoons extra-virgin olive oil, plus more for greasing
- 4 heads red Belgian endive, cut in half lengthwise (use white if you can't find red)
- 1 carrot, peeled and finely chopped
- 1 rib celery, finely chopped
- 2 oz (60 g) pancetta, minced
- 1 clove garlic, minced
- Fine sea salt and freshly ground black pepper
- ¼ cup (2 fl oz/60 ml) dry white wine
- 1 cup (7 oz/220 g) canned diced tomatoes
- ½ cup (2 oz/60 g) freshly grated Parmigiano-Reggiano cheese

1. Preheat the oven to 350°F (175°C). Lightly oil an 8-inch (20-cm) square baking dish.
2. In a large frying pan, heat the olive oil over medium heat. Arrange the endive halves in the dish, cut side down. Cook, turning once, until browned on both sides, about 4 minutes per side. Using a slotted spatula, transfer the endive halves to the prepared dish, cut side up.
3. Add the carrot, celery, pancetta, and garlic to the frying pan and sauté over medium heat until the vegetables have begun to soften, about 5 minutes. Add ½ teaspoon salt and pepper to taste and sauté until the vegetables are soft and the pancetta is starting to crisp, about 5 minutes. Raise the heat to medium-high and pour in the wine. Cook until most of the wine has evaporated, about 1 minute. Stir in the tomatoes and bring to a simmer. Reduce the heat to medium-low and cook until the sauce has thickened, about 10 minutes.
4. Spoon the sauce over the endive halves, cover with aluminum foil, and bake for 1 hour. Uncover and sprinkle with the cheese, then bake, uncovered, until the top is golden brown, about 20 minutes longer. Let cool for 5 minutes, then serve.

SWISS CHARD POTATOES

Prep time: 10 minutes | Cook time: **36 minutes** | Serves **6**

- 2 pounds Swiss chard
- 4 quarts salted water
- 3 medium Idaho potatoes (about 1¼ pounds), peeled and cut crosswise into 4 pieces
- ¼ cup extra-virgin olive oil
- 4 cloves garlic, crushed and peeled
- Salt and freshly ground black pepper

1. To prepare the chard: Trim the ends from the stems. Cut off and discard any wilted or yellow parts of the leaves. Strip the stems from the leaves, and cut the stems into ½-inch lengths. Cut the leaves in half lengthwise, then crosswise into ½-inch strips. Wash the leaf and stem pieces thoroughly, then drain them well.
2. Bring the salted water to a boil in a large pot. Add the potatoes, and cook 20 minutes, until tender. Add the Swiss chard stems. After another 10 minutes add the leaves, then cook all until the vegetables are very tender, an additional 5 minutes. Drain in a colander.
3. Heat 2 tablespoons of the olive oil in a large skillet over medium heat. Add the garlic, and cook just until it begins to brown, about 1 minute. Add the Swiss chard and potatoes, and season them lightly with salt and pepper. Cook, stirring and mashing the potatoes, until the liquid is evaporated and the potatoes are coarsely mashed. If the potatoes begin to brown, adjust the level of heat to medium-low and continue stirring. Add the remaining 2 tablespoons olive oil, and season to taste with salt and pepper, stir, and serve hot.

VEGETABLE CASSEROLE

Prep time: **10 minutes** | Cook time: **36 minutes** | Serves **6**

- 1/2 cup plus 2 tablespoons olive oil
- 1 medium-size eggplant, coarsely chopped
- 1 medium-size zucchini, coarsely chopped
- 1/2 pound cremini or white mushrooms, stems discarded and caps coarsely chopped
- 1/2 cup coarsely chopped onions
- Kosher salt and freshly ground black pepper
- 1 cup Sailor's-Style Sauce or your own favorite marinara sauce
- 1/4 cup freshly grated Parmesan or pecorino Romano cheese

1. Preheat the oven to 350° F.
2. Warm 1/4 cup of the olive oil in a medium-size sauté pan set over medium heat. Add the eggplant and cook, stirring, until softened, about 5 minutes. Use a slotted spoon to transfer the eggplant to a medium-size casserole dish and set aside. Add 2 more tablespoons of the olive oil and the zucchini to the sauté pan and cook until the center is softened and the rind still firm, about 3 minutes. Transfer the zucchini to the casserole with a slotted spoon and set aside. Finally, add the remaining 2 tablespoons olive oil and the onions to the sauté pan and cook until softened, about 3 minutes. Transfer to the casserole with a slotted spoon.
3. Season the vegetables with salt and pepper. Add the marinara sauce and toss to distribute the sauce evenly among the vegetables. Sprinkle with the cheese. Bake until the vegetables are cooked through, about 25 minutes. Serve immediately.

BRAISED LEEKS WITH PARMESAN CHEESE

Prep time: **10 minutes** | Cook time: **25 minutes** | Serves **4**

- 4 large or 6 medium leeks
- 3 tablespoons butter
- salt
- 3 tablespoons freshly grated parmigiano-reggiano cheese

1. Pull off any yellow or withered leaves from the leeks. Trim away the roots from the bulbous end. Do not cut off the green tops. Cut each leek lengthwise in two. Wash the leeks very thoroughly under cold running water, spreading the tops with your hands to make sure any hidden bits of grit are washed away.
2. Put the leeks in a pan just broad or long enough so that they can lie flat and straight. Add the butter, salt, and enough water to cover, put a lid on the pan, and turn on the heat to medium low. Cook until the thickest part of the leeks feels tender when prodded with a fork, about 15 to 25 minutes, depending on the vegetable's youth and freshness. Turn them from time to time while they cook.
3. When done, uncover the pan, turn the heat up to high, and boil away all the watery juices in the pan. In the process the leeks should become lightly browned. Before removing from heat, add the grated Parmesan, turn the leeks over once or twice, then transfer to a warm platter and serve at once.

WHITE WINE–BRAISED BROCCOLI RABE WITH OLIVES

Prep time: **10 minutes** | Cook time: **32 minutes** | Serves **4**

- 1¼ lb (625 g) rapini (broccoli rabe), tough stems removed
- 2 large cloves garlic, minced
- 3 tablespoons extra-virgin olive oil
- ½ cup (2½ oz/75 g) pitted cured black olives, coarsely chopped
- 2 imported Italian or Spanish anchovy fillets, finely chopped
- 1 small fresh hot chile, seeded and minced, or a generous pinch of red pepper flakes
- 1 cup (8 fl oz/250 ml) dry white wine
- Fine sea salt

1. Bring a large saucepan of water to a boil over high heat. Add the rapini and cook just until wilted, 3–4 minutes. Drain and let cool for 5 minutes, then chop very coarsely.

2. In a large frying pan over medium-low heat, warm the garlic in the olive oil, stirring often, until the garlic is softened but not browned, about 7 minutes. Stir in the olives, anchovies, and chile and sauté until fragrant, about 1 minute.

3. Raise the heat to medium and add the rapini to the pan, stirring to combine the greens with the olives and anchovies. Pour in the wine, raise the heat to medium-high, and bring to a simmer. Reduce the heat to medium-low, cover partially, and braise until the rapini is tender and most of the liquid has been absorbed, 15–20 minutes. Season with salt, if needed, and serve right away.

BREADED FRIED FINOCCHIO

Prep time: **10 minutes** | Cook time: **25 minutes** | Serves **4-6**

- 3 finocchi
- 2 eggs
- 1½ cups unflavored bread crumbs, lightly toasted, spread on a plate
- vegetable oil
- salt

1. Trim, slice, and wash the finocchio as described in Braised Finocchio with Olive Oil.

2. Bring 3 quarts of water to a boil, then drop in the sliced finocchio. Cook at a moderate boil until the butt end of the slice feels tender, but firm when prodded with a fork. Drain, and set aside to cool.

3. Beat the eggs with a fork in a deep dish or small bowl.

4. Dip the cooled, parboiled finocchio slices in the beaten egg, letting excess egg flow back into the dish, then turn it in the bread crumbs, coating both sides. Press the bread crumbs onto each slice with the palm of your hand until your hand feels dry and the crumbs are sticking firmly to the finocchio.

5. Pour enough oil into a frying pan to come ½ inch up the sides. When you think the oil is quite hot, test it by dipping into it the end of one of the slices. If it sizzles, the oil is ready for frying. Slip as many slices of finocchio into the pan as will fit loosely without overlapping. Cook until they form a crisp, golden brown crust on one side, then turn them and do the other side. When both sides are done, use a slotted spoon or spatula to transfer them to a cooling rack to drain or to a platter lined with paper towels. Repeat the procedure until all the finocchio is done. Sprinkle with salt and serve at once.

SAUTÉED MIXED GREENS WITH OLIVE OIL AND GARLIC

Prep time: **10 minutes** | Cook time: **35 minutes** | Serves **6**

- 1 pound fresh spinach or swiss chard
- ½ pound cime di rapa, also called rapini or broccoletti di rapa
- 1-pound head Savoy cabbage
- salt
- ¼ cup extra virgin olive oil
- 1 tablespoon chopped garlic
- black pepper, ground fresh from the mill

1. Snap off the thicker, older stems from the spinach leaves, or detach the broadest, more mature stalks from the Swiss chard and soak either green in a basin filled with cold water. Scoop up the spinach or chard, empty out the water together with any soil, refill the basin with fresh cold water, and put the green back in to soak. Repeat the operation several times until you find no more soil settling to the bottom of the basin.
2. In a separate basin soak the cime di rapa in exactly the same manner.
3. Pull off and discard the darkest outer leaves of the Savoy cabbage. Cut off the butt end of the stem, and cut the head into 4 parts.
4. Bring 3 to 4 quarts water to a boil, add 1 tablespoon salt, and put in the cime di rapa. Put a lid on the pot, setting it ajar, and cook until tender, about 8 to 12 minutes, depending on the green's freshness and youth. Drain and set aside. Refill the pot with fresh water, and if using Swiss chard, cook it in the same manner. After draining the chard, refill the pot and cook the cabbage using the same procedure, except that you must omit the salt. Cook the cabbage until the thickest part of the head is easily pierced by a fork, about 15 to 20 minutes.
5. If using spinach, cook it in a covered pan with ½ tablespoon salt and just the moisture that clings to its leaves from the soak. Cook until tender, about 10 minutes or more, depending on the spinach. Drain and set aside.
6. Gently but firmly squeeze all the moisture you can out of all the greens. Chop them together to a rather coarse consistency.
7. Put the oil and garlic in a large sauté pan, and turn on the heat to medium. Cook and stir the garlic until it becomes colored a very pale gold, then put in all the chopped greens. Add salt and pepper and turn them over completely 3 or 4 times to coat them well. Cook for 10 to 15 minutes, turning the greens frequently. Taste and correct for salt. Serve promptly.

OLIVE OIL MASHED POTATOES

Prep time: **10 minutes** | Cook time: **30 minutes** | Serves **4**

- 1 pound Idaho or Yukon Gold potatoes, scrubbed but unpeeled
- Salt
- ¼ cup extra-virgin olive oil
- Freshly ground pepper, preferably white

1. Pour enough cold water over the potatoes in a large saucepan to cover them by a few inches. Season the water wi4th salt, and bring to a boil. Cook until the potatoes are tender but still hold their shape, 15 to 30 minutes, depending on the size and shape of the potatoes. Drain the potatoes, and let stand until cool enough to handle.
2. Peel the potatoes, and pass them through a ricer or a food mill with a fine disc. Gently stir in the olive oil, and season them to taste with salt and pepper. Serve hot.

EGGPLANT PARMIGIANA

Prep time: **10 minutes** | Cook time: **45 minutes** | Serves **4 to 6**

- 2 medium eggplants
- ¾ cup all-purpose flour
- Salt
- Freshly ground black pepper
- 3–4 tablespoons extra-virgin olive oil, for sautéing
- 2 cups tomato sauce
- ½ cup grated Parmesan
- 8 ounces mozzarella, shredded

1. Preheat the oven to 375°F.

2. Peel eggplants with a potato peeler to remove the thin purply skin. Cut eggplants into ¼-inch rounds.

3. Place the flour in a medium-large shallow bowl, and season well with salt and pepper. Heat 3 to 4 tablespoons of oil in a large frying pan. When hot, dredge eggplant slices in flour, shake off excess, and fry until golden on each side, 3 to 4 minutes. Repeat with the rest of the slices, adding more olive oil to the pan if needed. Drain slices on a paper-towel-lined plate.

4. Add a thin layer of tomato sauce to a 9-by-13-inch casserole dish (or similar). Place one layer of eggplant slices at bottom. Coat lightly with tomato sauce. Sprinkle on some grated Parmesan and shredded mozzarella. Add another layer of eggplant; coat with a little sauce; add more of the cheeses. Repeat until all the slices and cheeses are used.

5. Bake for about 30 minutes until the casserole is bubbling and the cheeses are melted. Let stand 10 to 15 minutes before cutting into squares and serving.

BRAISED ARTICHOKES AND LEEKS

Prep time: **10 minutes** | Cook time: **35 minutes** | Serves **6**

- 3 large globe artichokes or 5 or 6 medium size
- ½ lemon
- 4 large leeks, about 1¾ inches thick, or 6 smaller ones
- ¼ cup extra virgin olive oil
- salt
- black pepper, ground fresh from the mill

1. Cut the trimmed artichokes into 1-inch wedges and pare and split the stems . As you work, rub the cut artichokes with the lemon to keep them from turning black.

2. Trim away the roots of the leeks, any of their leaves that are blemished, and about 1 inch off their green tops. Slice the leeks in half lengthwise, then cut them into pieces about 2 or 3 inches long.

3. Choose a heavy-bottomed or enameled cast-iron pot just large enough to accommodate all the ingredients, put in the leeks, the olive oil, and sufficient water to come 1 inch up the sides of the pan. Turn on the heat to medium, cover tightly, and cook at a steady simmer until the leeks are tender.

4. Add the artichoke wedges, salt, pepper, and, if necessary, 2 or 3 tablespoons water. Cover again and cook until the artichokes feel very tender at their thickest point when prodded with a fork, about 30 minutes or more, very much depending on the artichokes. While the artichokes are cooking, add 2 or 3 tablespoons of water if you find that there is not enough liquid. When they are done, taste and correct for salt. If you should find, once the artichokes are cooked, that the juices in the pot are watery, uncover, raise the heat to high, and quickly boil them away.

BRAISED FINOCCHIO WITH OLIVE OIL

Prep time: **10 minutes** | Cook time: **25 minutes** | Serves **4**

- 3 large finocchi or 4 to 5 smaller ones
- ⅓ cup extra virgin olive oil
- salt

1. Cut the finocchio tops where they meet the bulb and discard them. Detach and discard any of the bulb's outer parts that may be bruised or discolored. Slice off about ⅛ inch from the butt end. Cut the bulb vertically into slices somewhat less than ½ inch thick. Wash the slices in several changes of cold water.

2. Put the finocchio and the olive oil in a large saucepan, add just enough water to cover, and turn on the heat to medium. Do not put a lid on the pot. Cook, turning the slices over from time to time, until the finocchio becomes colored a glossy, pale gold and feels tender when prodded with a fork. Bear in mind that the butt end of the slice should be firm compared with the softer upper part of the slice. It should take between 25 and 40 minutes, depending on the freshness of the finocchio. If while cooking you find the liquid in the pan becoming insufficient, add up to   cup water. By the time the finocchio is done, all the water must be absorbed. Add salt, toss the slices once or twice, then transfer the contents of the pan to a warm platter and serve at once.

ROASTED VEGETABLES

Prep time: **10 minutes** | Cook time: **30 minutes** | Serves **8**

- 1 tablespoon coarsely chopped fresh basil leaves
- 1 tablespoon chopped fresh rosemary leaves
- 1 tablespoon chopped fresh Italian, flat leafed parsley
- 1 tablespoon chopped fresh thyme leaves
- 2 large Yukon Gold or Red Bliss potatoes, peeled, cut in half, and then into 2-inch pieces
- 2 large carrots, peeled, cut in half, and then into 1-inch pieces
- 4 cloves garlic, cut in half
- Kosher salt and freshly ground black pepper
- 3 tablespoons Sailor's-Style Sauce or your own favorite marinara sauce (optional)
- 1/2 cup olive oil
- 1 large yellow or green zucchini, cut in half, and then into 1-inch pieces
- 1 large sweet potato, peeled, cut in half, and then into 1-inch pieces
- 1 medium-size butternut squash, peeled, cut in half, seeded, and then cut into 1-inch pieces
- 1 tablespoon balsamic vinegar
- 1 tablespoon extra virgin olive oil

1. 1. Preheat the oven to 350° F.
2. 2. In small bowl, combine the chopped herbs. Set aside.
3. 3. In a large casserole or baking dish, toss the potatoes and carrots with half of the herb mixture. Stir in the garlic and season with salt and pepper. Stir in the marinara sauce, if using, and 1/4 cup of the olive oil. Bake, stirring occasionally, until the potatoes begin to brown and soften, about 30 minutes.
4. 4. Add the zucchini, sweet potato, butternut squash, the remaining herbs, and 1/4 cup olive oil. Toss to coat evenly. Continue baking, stirring occasionally, until all of the vegetables are browned but firm and cooked through, about 1 hour. Drizzle the vinegar and extra virgin olive oil over the vegetables and toss. Serve immediately.

ROASTED SWEET BABY PEPPERS WITH OREGANO

Prep time: **10 minutes** | Cook time: **25 minutes** | Serves **4 to 6**

- 1 pound baby bell peppers (usually in assorted colors)
- 3 tablespoons extra-virgin olive oil
- 1 teaspoon dried oregano
- Salt
- Freshly ground black pepper
- Leaves from 2 or 3 sprigs fresh oregano, minced

1. Preheat the oven to 400°F.
2. Put peppers in a medium mixing bowl. Drizzle them with olive oil and toss to coat the peppers. Sprinkle them with dried oregano. Season with salt and pepper. Mix to combine.
3. Lay peppers out in a single layer on a foil-lined, lightly oiled sheet pan.
4. Roast for 20 to 25 minutes, until softened and beginning to brown.
5. Transfer peppers to a serving platter. Sprinkle with fresh oregano. Serve.

ASPARAGUS & HAZELNUT ROAST

Prep time: **10 minutes** | Cook time: **25 minutes** | Serves **4**

- 2 tbsp olive oil
- 1 lb asparagus, trimmed
- ¼ cup hazelnuts, chopped
- 1 lemon, juiced and zested
- Salt and black pepper to taste
- ½ tsp red pepper flakes

1. Preheat oven to 420 F.
2. Arrange the asparagus on a baking sheet.
3. Combine olive oil, lemon zest, lemon juice, salt, hazelnuts, and black pepper in a bowl and mix well.
4. Pour the mixture over the asparagus.
5. Place in the oven and roast for 15-20 minutes until tender and lightly charred.
6. Serve topped with red pepper flakes.

TOMATO-BRAISED ROMANO BEANS WITH BASIL

Prep time: **10 minutes** | Cook time: **33 minutes** | Serves **4**

- 2 tablespoons extra-virgin olive oil
- 2 cloves garlic, crushed flat but left whole
- 1 lb (500 g) romano beans (flat green beans), stem ends removed, cut in half crosswise
- 2 cups (14 oz/440 g) canned diced tomatoes
- 1 small fresh hot chile, seeded and minced, or a generous pinch of red pepper flakes
- Fine sea salt
- 2 tablespoons coarsely chopped fresh basil

1. In a large frying pan over medium-low heat, combine the olive oil and garlic and heat until the garlic begins to sizzle, about 3 minutes. Press on the garlic with the back of a wooden spoon or spatula to release its aroma. Do not let the garlic brown or it will become bitter.
2. Add the beans to the pan and stir to coat them with the oil. Stir in the tomatoes, chile, and ½ teaspoon salt. Raise the heat to medium and bring to a simmer, then reduce the heat to low and simmer gently until the beans are tender but not mushy and the sauce has thickened, 25–30 minutes. Remove from the heat and remove and discard the garlic. Stir in the basil. Serve right away.
3. Season with salt and pepper and sprinkle in the vinegar. Cook, tossing occasionally, until the greens are just tender, 7–8 minutes. They should still be a bit crunchy but no longer taste raw.
4. Pile the kale in a serving bowl or on a serving platter and sprinkle the pancetta on top. Serve hot or warm.

BRAISED ARTICHOKES AND POTATOES

Prep time: 10 minutes | Cook time: 25 minutes | Serves 4-6

- 2 large globe artichokes
- ½ lemon
- 1 pound potatoes
- ⅓ cup onion chopped coarse
- ¼ cup extra virgin olive oil
- ¼ teaspoon garlic chopped very fine
- salt
- black pepper, ground fresh from the mill
- 1 tablespoon chopped parsley

1. Cut the trimmed artichokes into 1-inch wedges, and trim and split the stems . As you work, rub the cut artichokes with the lemon to keep them from turning black.

2. Peel the potatoes, wash them in cold water, and cut them into small wedges about ¾ inch thick at their broadest point.

3. Choose a heavy-bottomed or enameled cast-iron pot just large enough to accommodate all the ingredients, put in the chopped onion and olive oil, and turn on the heat to medium high. Cook and stir the onion until it becomes translucent, but not colored, then add the garlic. Cook the garlic until it becomes colored a light gold, then put in the potatoes, the artichoke wedges and stems, salt, pepper, and parsley, and cook long enough to turn over all the ingredients 2 or 3 times.

4. Add ¼ cup water, adjust heat to cook at a steady, but gentle simmer, and cover tightly. Cook until both the potatoes and artichokes feel tender when prodded with a fork, approximately 40 minutes, depending mostly on the potatoes. While cooking, add 2 or 3 tablespoons of water if you find that there is not enough liquid in the pot. Taste and correct for salt before serving.

SAUTÉED SWISS CHARD WITH RADICCHIO AND LEEK

Prep time: 15 minutes | Cook time: 8 minutes | Serves 4 to 6

- 1 leek
- 1 bunch Swiss chard (about 10 stalks)
- ½ head radicchio (about ⅓ pound)
- 2 tablespoons extra-virgin olive oil, for sautéing
- Salt and freshly ground black pepper

1. Cut off the green end of the leek; use only the white part. Cut off the root. Cut leek in half lengthwise, and rinse under cool water, thumbing through the layers to clean well. Pat dry. Cut lengthwise again to get 4 long quarters. Cut across quarters into thin, small slices.

2. Rinse the Swiss chard and pat it dry. Gently rip the leaves of the Swiss chard from the ribs. (Discard ribs.) Tear or cut leaves into bite-size pieces. Cut radicchio into thin slices.

3. Heat 2 tablespoons of olive oil in a large sauté pan. When hot, add the cut-up leek. Sauté until softened and beginning to turn golden, about 4 minutes. Add the Swiss chard and radicchio. Cook at a lively simmer for 2 to 3 minutes, until leafy vegetables have wilted. Season with salt and pepper to taste. Serve.

CHAPTER 11: DESSERTS AND DRINKS

HOME-STYLE FRUIT CUPS

Prep time: **10 minutes** | Cook time: **none** | Serves **4**

- 1 cup orange juice
- ½ cup watermelon cubes
- 1 ½ cups grapes, halved
- 1 cup chopped cantaloupe
- ½ cup cherries, chopped
- 1 peach, chopped
- ½ tsp ground cinnamon

1. Combine the watermelon cubes, grapes, cherries, cantaloupe, and peach in a bowl.
2. Add in the orange juice and mix well.
3. Share into dessert cups, dust with cinnamon, and serve.

MINTY SICILIAN ALMOND GRANITA

Prep time: **10 minutes** | Cook time: **none** | Serves **4**

- 4 small oranges, chopped
- ½ tsp almond extract
- 2 tbsp lemon juice
- 1 cup orange juice
- ¼ cup honey
- Fresh mint leaves for garnish

1. In a food processor, mix the oranges, orange juice, honey, almond extract, and lemon juice.
2. Pulse until smooth.
3. Pour in a dip dish and freeze for 1 hour.
4. Mix with a fork and freeze for 30 minutes more.
5. Repeat a couple of times.
6. Pour into dessert glasses and garnish with basil leaves.
7. Serve.

HOMEMADE SAMBUCA

Prep time: **30 minutes** | Cook time: **45 minutes** | Makes about 3¼ cups (12 to 14 servings)

- 1½ cups 190-proof grain alcohol or neutral spirit, such as everclear
- ½ cup whole star anise
- 2 tablespoons dried elderberries (optional; see note)
- 2 cups sugar
- ⅛ teaspoon kosher salt
- espresso beans (optional), for serving

1. In a clean, dry 32-ounce glass jar, combine the alcohol, star anise, and elderberries (if using). Seal tightly and let steep at room temperature in a cool, dry place for at least 1 month and up to 1 year.
2. When the liquid is ready, in a small saucepan, combine the sugar, salt, and 2¼ cups water and bring to a boil over medium-high heat. Remove from the heat and stir well, ensuring all the sugar is melted. Transfer to a heatproof bowl and place in the refrigerator to cool.
3. Strain the alcohol infusion through a fine-mesh sieve into a clean, dry bowl. Add the chilled sugar syrup and whisk well to combine. Using a funnel, transfer to a decorative bottle. Store in the freezer.
4. Serve sambuca chilled in cordial glasses, with 2 espresso beans per glass, if desired. Sambuca keeps indefinitely in the freezer.

SIMPLE RICOTTA CAKE

Prep time: **10 minutes** | Cook time: **none** |
Serves **8**

- 2 cups ricotta cheese
- 1 1/2 tablespoons butter, softened
- 5 large eggs
- 3 tablespoons all-purpose flour
- 11/4 cups confectioners' sugar
- 2 tablespoons pure vanilla extract
- 1 tablespoon dark rum (such as Myers's) (optional)
- 2 cups heavy cream
- 1/2 teaspoon grated lemon or orange zest

1. If the ricotta cheese is very wet, place it in a fine-mesh sieve lined with cheesecloth. Place the sieve over a bowl, refrigerate, and drain the ricotta for 2 hours.
2. Preheat the oven to 325° F. Completely line an 8-inch springform pan with two overlapping layers of aluminum foil. Grease the foil with the softened butter and dust lightly with flour, set aside.
3. Place the eggs in a large bowl. with an electric mixer set on high speed, beat the eggs just to combine, about 10 seconds. Add the ricotta, flour, sugar, vanilla, and rum, if using, and beat just to combine. Reduce the mixer speed to low and gradually add the cream. Stir in the zest.
4. Pour the mixture into the prepared springform pan, and bake until the edges of the cake are firm and the top is golden brown, about 1 hour. (If the top begins to brown too quickly, cover the pan with aluminum foil and continue to bake.) Remove the pan from the oven, set it on a wire rack, and allow to cool for 3 to 4 hours. Remove the outer ring of the pan and cut away the foil. Cover and refrigerate the cake for at least 3 hours before serving.

PINE NUT COOKIES

Prep time: **5 minutes** | Cook time: **10 minutes** |
Makes about 3 dozen cookies

- ½ cup (1 stick) unsalted butter, at room temperature
- ½ cup plus 2 tablespoons sugar
- 1 teaspoon pure vanilla extract
- 1 teaspoon ground fennel seed
- ¼ teaspoon salt
- 1 large egg
- 1¼ cups all-purpose flour
- ¼ cup pine nuts

1. In a large bowl, beat the butter, sugar, vanilla, ground fennel seed, and salt with an electric mixer until light and fluffy.
2. Beat in the egg. Add the flour and mix just until blended.
3. Transfer the dough to a sheet of plastic wrap and shape into an 8-inch-long log.
4. Wrap the dough in plastic and refrigerate for 2 hours.
5. Preheat the oven to 350 degrees F.
6. Line 2 heavy, large baking sheets with parchment paper.
7. Cut the dough log crosswise into ⅛- to ¼-inch-thick slices.
8. Transfer the cookies to the prepared baking sheets, spacing evenly apart.
9. Press the pine nuts decoratively atop the cookies, and bake until the cookies are golden around the edges, about 15 minutes.
10. Store airtight at room temperature

STUFFED BAKED APPLES

Prep time: **10 minutes** | Cook time: **40 minutes** | Serves **4**

- 2 tbsp brown sugar
- 4 apples, cored
- ¼ cup chopped pecans
- 1 tsp ground cinnamon
- ¼ tsp ground nutmeg
- ¼ tsp ground ginger

1. Preheat your oven to 375 F.
2. Arrange the apples cut-side up on a baking dish.
3. Combine pecans, ginger, cinnamon, brown sugar, and nutmeg in a bowl.
4. Scoop the mixture into the apples and bake for 35-40 minutes until golden brown.

ANISE SPONGE

Prep time: **5 minutes** | Cook time: **30 minutes** | Serves **4**

- 1 cup all-purpose flour
- 2 tablespoons cornstarch
- 1 teaspoon baking powder
- ¼ teaspoon table salt
- 2 large eggs
- ¾ cup sugar
- 2 teaspoons anise extract

1. Preheat the oven to 350°F, and line a baking sheet with parchment paper.
2. In a bowl, mix together the flour, cornstarch, baking powder, and salt.
3. with a mixer on high speed, beat the eggs and sugar together for several minutes. Mix in the anise extract.
4. with a rubber spatula, add the flour mixture and blend just until combined. The batter will be soft.

TOMATOES STUFFED WITH SHRIMP

Prep time: **10 minutes** | Cook time: **35 minutes** | Serves **6**

- 6 large, round, ripe firm tomatoes
- salt
- 1 tablespoon red wine vinegar
- ¾ pound small raw shrimp in the shell
- Mayonnaise, made as directed on , using the yolk of 1 large egg, ½ cup vegetable oil, and 2½ to 3 tablespoons freshly squeezed lemon juice
- 1½ tablespoons capers, soaked and rinsed if packed in salt, drained if packed in vinegar
- 1 teaspoon English or Dijon-style mustard
- parsley

1. Slice the tops off the tomatoes. with a small spoon, possibly a serrated grapefruit spoon, scoop out all the seeds, and remove some of the dividing walls, leaving 3 or 4 large sections. Don't squeeze the tomato at any time. Sprinkle with salt, and turn the tomatoes upside down on a platter to let excess liquid drain out.
2. Rinse the shrimp in cold water. Fill a pot with 2 quarts of water. Add the vinegar and 1 tablespoon of salt, and bring to a boil. Drop in the shrimp and cook for just 1 minute (or more, depending on their size) after the water returns to a boil. Drain, shell, and devein the shrimp. Set aside to cool completely.
3. Set aside 6 of the best-looking, most regularly formed shrimp. Chop the rest not too fine, put them in a bowl, and mix them with the mayonnaise, capers, and mustard.
4. Shake off the excess liquid from the tomatoes without squeezing them. Stuff to the top with the shrimp mixture. Garnish each tomato with a whole shrimp and 1 or 2 parsley leaves. Serve at room temperature or even just slightly chilled.

85

ALMOND CAKE

Prep time: **5 minutes** | Cook time: **10 minutes** | Makes 1 (8-inch) round cake

- ½ cup fine yellow cornmeal
- ½ cup cake flour
- 1 teaspoon baking powder
- ½ cup (1 stick) unsalted butter, at room temperature
- ¼ cup almond paste, cut into small pieces
- ½ teaspoon pure vanilla extract
- 1¼ cups confectioners' sugar, plus more for dusting
- 4 large egg yolks
- 2 large eggs
- ¼ cup sour cream

1. Position the rack in the center of the oven and preheat the oven to 350 degrees F.
2. Butter and flour an 8-inch round cake pan.
3. In a medium bowl, whisk together the cornmeal, cake flour, and baking powder.
4. Using a stand mixer with a paddle attachment, beat the butter and almond paste on high speed until smooth, about 3 minutes.
5. Reduce the speed to low and beat in the vanilla extract.
6. Gradually add 1¼ cups of confectioners' sugar, beating until the mixture is light and fluffy, about 3 minutes.
7. Increase the speed to high and beat in the egg yolks and whole eggs, one at a time.
8. Reduce the speed to medium and add the sour cream and dry ingredients and mix until just incorporated.
9. Pour the batter into the prepared cake pan and smooth the surface with a spatula.
10. Bake until the cake is golden and pulls away from the sides of the pan, about 35 minutes.
11. Transfer the pan to a wire rack and let cool.
12. Remove the cake from the pan and dust with more confectioners' sugar. (the cake can be made 1 day ahead.
13. Store airtight in a plastic container.) Cut the cake into wedges and serve.

TUSCAN CANTUCCI

Prep time: **15 minutes** | Cook time: **35 to 40 minutes** | Serves **4 to 6**

- 2 cups all-purpose flour
- 1 cup sugar
- 1 teaspoon baking powder
- ¼ teaspoon salt
- 2 large eggs plus 1 large egg yolk, lightly beaten
- Zest of 1 large orange
- 1 cup hazelnuts or almonds, roughly chopped

1. Preheat the oven to 350°F. Line a baking sheet with parchment paper.
2. On a clean surface, mix the flour, sugar, baking powder, and salt by stirring with a fork.
3. Make a well in the middle, and add the eggs and zest. Using a fork or your fingers, start incorporating some of the flour into the egg, little by little, until a dough is formed.
4. Add the nuts and mix into the dough until well incorporated. Divide the dough in half and form two logs. Place them on the baking sheet several inches apart.
5. Bake for 22 to 25 minutes. Remove the logs from the oven and cool for 10 minutes. Using a serrated knife, cut the logs diagonally into slices, place them back on the baking sheet, cut-side down, lower the oven temperature to 325°F, and bake for 10 to 15 more minutes, turning halfway through so they toast evenly.

BELLINI COCKTAIL

Prep time: **10 minutes** | Cook time: **none** | Serves **4**

- 2 large or 3 medium white peaches, ripe, refrigerated, plus more for serving
- 2 teaspoons fresh lemon juice
- 1 teaspoon sugar (optional)
- 2 cups Prosecco, refrigerated

1. Peel the peaches, remove the pits, cut in pieces, and use a blender to blend with the lemon juice and sugar, if using. Strain.
2. Divide the pureed peach among 4 chilled champagne glasses. It should fill about one-third of each glass. Slowly top with ½ cup cold Prosecco, per cup. Stir once right before serving.
3. Decorate each glass with a peach slice, peel on, if you'd like.

FRANGELICO NUT BARS

Prep time: **10 minutes** | Cook time: **none** | Serves **4**

- 2 tbsp olive oil
- ¼ cup shredded coconut
- 1 cup pistachios
- ½ tsp Amaretto liqueur
- 1 cup almonds
- 2 cups dates, pitted
- ¼ cup cocoa powder

1. In a food processor, blend the pistachios, dates, almonds, olive oil, Amaretto liqueur, and cocoa powder until well minced.
2. Make tablespoon-size balls out of the mixture.
3. Roll the balls in the shredded coconut to coat.
4. Serve chilled.

NOCINO WITH ESPRESSO BEANS & LEMON

Prep time: **30 minutes** | Cook time: **45 minutes** | Makes about 7½ cups

- 1 (750 ml) bottle 190-proof grain alcohol or neutral spirit, such as everclear
- 20 green walnuts, cut into quarters
- 6 to 8 strips of lemon zest (from 1 lemon)
- ¼ cup medium or dark roast coffee beans
- 2 cinnamon sticks
- 2 cups sugar
- ⅛ teaspoon kosher salt

1. Clean and dry a glass jar large enough to accommodate all the ingredients without being filled to the brim—there should be about 2 inches of space for air. A gallon jar usually does the trick. Add the alcohol, walnuts, lemon zest, coffee beans, and cinnamon sticks to the jar, seal tightly, and let steep at room temperature in a cool, dry place for at least 4 months and up to 1 year. The liquid will turn very dark brown in color.
2. When the nocino has steeped sufficiently, in a small saucepan, combine the sugar, salt, and 2 cups water and bring to a boil over medium-high heat. Remove from the heat and stir well, ensuring all the sugar is melted. Transfer to a heatproof bowl and place in the refrigerator to cool.
3. Strain the alcohol infusion through a fine-mesh sieve into a clean, dry bowl. Add the chilled sugar syrup and whisk well to combine. Using a funnel, transfer to a decorative bottle. Store in the freezer.
4. Serve nocino chilled in cordial glasses. Nocino keeps indefinitely in the freezer.

MUSHROOM, PARMESAN CHEESE, AND WHITE TRUFFLE SALAD

Prep time: **10 minutes** | Cook time: **25 minutes** | Serves **4**

- ½ pound firm, sound fresh mushrooms (see introductory note above)
- 1 to 2 tablespoons freshly squeezed lemon juice
- ⅔ cup celery cut crosswise into ¼-inch slices
- ⅔ cup parmigiano-reggiano cheese, shaved into flakes with a vegetable peeler or on a mandoline
- Optional:
- a 1-ounce or larger white truffle
- 3 tablespoons extra virgin olive oil
- salt
- black pepper, ground fresh from the mill

1. Wash the mushrooms quickly under cold running water. Do not let them soak. Pat them thoroughly dry with a cloth or paper towels. Cut them into very thin slices, about ⅛ inch thick, slicing them lengthwise so that the center slices have a part of both the stem and the cap.
2. Put the sliced mushrooms in a shallow bowl or platter and toss immediately with the lemon juice to keep them white. Add the sliced celery and the flakes of Parmesan cheese. If you own a truffle slicer, use it to slice the optional white truffle very thin into the bowl. Otherwise, use a vegetable peeler in a light sawing motion.
3. Toss with the olive oil, salt, and pepper. Serve promptly.

CHOCOLATE AMARETTI CAKE

Prep time: **5 minutes** | Cook time: **10 minutes** | Serves **6**

- butter-flavored nonstick cooking spray
- ¾ cup semisweet chocolate chips
- 1 cup slivered almonds
- 1 cup (about 2 ounces) baby amaretti cookies
- ½ cup unsalted butter (1 stick), at room temperature
- ⅔ cup sugar
- 2 teaspoons grated orange zest (from approximately 1 orange)
- 4 large eggs
- about 2 tablespoons unsweetened cocoa powder, for sifting

1. Preheat the oven to 350 degrees F.
2. Spray a 9-inch springform pan with nonstick spray and refrigerate.
3. In a small bowl, microwave the chocolate chips, stirring every 30 seconds, until melted and smooth, about 2 minutes.
4. In a food processor, combine the almonds and cookies, and pulse until finely ground.
5. Transfer to a bowl. Add the butter, sugar, and orange zest to the processor and blend until creamy and smooth.
6. with the machine running, add the eggs one at a time. Add the nut mixture and the melted chocolate.
7. Pulse until blended.
8. Pour the batter into the prepared pan.
9. Bake until the center puffs and a tester inserted into the center of the cake comes out clean, about 35 minutes.
10. Cool the cake in the pan for 15 minutes.
11. Transfer to a platter, sift the cocoa powder over, and serve.

RICCIARELLI

Prep time: 20 minutes | Cook time: 20 minutes | Serves 4 to 26

- 2½ cups toasted slivered almonds
- 2 teaspoons orange zest
- 1 cup confectioners' sugar, divided, plus more for dusting the cookies
- 2 large egg whites
- Pinch salt
- 1 teaspoon vanilla extract

1. Line two baking sheets with parchment paper. Set aside.
2. In the bowl of a food processor, combine the almonds, zest, and ½ cup of confectioners' sugar, and grind until the mixture resembles fine bread crumbs.
3. Use a hand mixer or stand mixer to mix the egg whites until soft peaks form. Gradually add the remaining ½ cup of sugar and salt, and continue mixing until stiff peaks form.
4. Fold the almond mixture and vanilla into the egg whites until combined. Drop a scoop of several tablespoons of the mixture onto the parchment paper, and with wet hands, construct a diamond shape. Repeat the process with the remaining batter. Let the cookies stand for at least 1 hour to dry out.
5. Preheat the oven to 350°F. Place the cookies on a baking sheet, about 1 inch apart, and bake for 15 to 20 minutes until the corners have darkened and the top is cracked. The center will be soft. Dust with confectioners' sugar.

TUSCAN BISCOTTI

Prep time: 10 minutes | Cook time: 40 minutes | Serves 4

- 31/4 cups all-purpose flour
- 21/2 teaspoons baking powder
- 1/2 teaspoon kosher salt
- 1/2 cup (1 stick) butter, softened
- 11/4 cups sugar
- 2 large eggs
- 2 large egg yolks
- 1/4 cup honey
- 1/2 teaspoon pure vanilla extract
- 1/4 teaspoon pure almond extract
- 1/4 teaspoon pure anise extract
- 1 cup unblanched whole almonds

1. In a medium-size bowl, mix the flour, baking powder, and salt. Set aside.
2. In a large bowl, with an electric mixer on high speed, cream the butter and sugar until light and fluffy, about 5 minutes. Add the whole eggs and yolks, one at a time, beating after each addition. Beat in the honey. Add the extracts and mix well. Reduce the speed to low and gradually beat in the dry ingredients. Stir in the almonds, mixing until they are well dispersed.
3. Turn the dough out onto a sheet of plastic wrap. Form the dough into a ball and flatten it slightly. Wrap and refrigerate until firm, about 30 minutes.
4. Preheat the oven to 350° F. Grease two baking sheets or line them with parchment paper, and set aside.
5. Remove the dough from the plastic wrap and divide it in half. On a lightly floured work surface, roll half the dough into a baguette-shaped log about 2 inches wide by 13 inches long, and transfer it to one of the prepared baking sheets. Repeat with the other half of the dough, transferring it to the other prepared baking sheet. Bake until firm and golden, about 30 minutes. Remove from the oven and allow to cool for 15 minutes.
6. Reduce the oven temperature to 250° F.
7. Transfer the cooled logs to a cutting board. Using a serrated knife, slice each log on the bias at 1/2-inch intervals. Place the slices on the baking sheet, cut side down. Bake until dry and lightly browned, about 10 minutes on each side. Transfer the biscotti to a wire rack and allow to cool completely. Store in an airtight container for up to 1 week.

TOASTED HAZELNUT & ORANGE LIQUEUR

Prep time: **30 minutes** | Cook time: **45 minutes** | **Makes about 2 1/3 cups (about 10 servings)**

- 3 cups blanched roasted unsalted hazelnuts
- 1 (750 ml) bottle 190-proof grain alcohol or neutral spirit, such as everclear
- 2 cups sugar
- ¼ teaspoon kosher salt
- ½ teaspoon vanilla bean paste
- strips of zest of 1 large orange, plus more for garnish, if desired
- ½ cup freshly squeezed orange juice, strained (from 1 large orange)

1. Preheat the oven to 400°F. Line a sheet pan with parchment paper or a silicone baking mat.
2. Spread the hazelnuts in a single layer on the lined pan. Place in the oven and toast until dark golden brown and the oil is released, about 12 minutes.
3. Carefully transfer the hazelnuts to a food processor and add the alcohol. Process for 20 to 30 seconds to form a puree.
4. Transfer to a clean, dry 64-ounce glass jar and let cool to room temperature. Seal tightly and let steep at room temperature in a cool, dry place for at least 1 month and up to 1 year. When ready, transfer to the freezer overnight.
5. When the liquid has frozen overnight, in a small saucepan, combine the sugar, salt, vanilla paste, orange zest, orange juice, and 2 cups water and bring to a boil over medium-high heat. Remove from the heat and stir well, ensuring all the sugar is melted. Strain the liquid through a fine-mesh sieve and refrigerate until cooled.
6. Remove the hazelnut-infused alcohol from the freezer. The nut mixture should have separated from the alcohol, sinking to the bottom and revealing the clarified alcohol on the top. Strain the alcohol infusion through a fine-mesh sieve into a clean, dry bowl.
7. Add the chilled vanilla-orange syrup and stir well to combine. Using a funnel, transfer to a decorative bottle. Store in the freezer.
8. Serve the liqueur chilled in cordial glasses. Garnish each glass with a twist of orange peel

TOMATOES STUFFED WITH TUNA

Prep time: **10 minutes** | Cook time: **35 minutes** | Serves **6**

- 6 large, round, ripe firm tomatoes
- salt
- 2 seven-ounce cans imported Italian tuna packed in olive oil
- Mayonnaise, made as directed on , using the yolk of 1 large egg, ½ cup vegetable oil, and 2 tablespoons freshly squeezed lemon juice
- 2 teaspoons English or Dijon-style mustard
- 1½ tablespoons capers, soaked and rinsed if packed in salt, drained if packed in vinegar
- garnishes as suggested below

1. Prepare the tomatoes for stuffing as described in Step 1 of the recipe for Tomatoes Stuffed with Shrimp on .
2. Put the tuna in a mixing bowl and mash it to a pulp with a fork. Add the mayonnaise, holding back 1 or 2 tablespoons, the mustard, and capers. Using the fork, mix to a uniform consistency. Taste and correct for salt.
3. Shake off the excess liquid from the tomatoes without squeezing them. Stuff to the top with the tuna mixture.
4. Spread the remaining mayonnaise on top of the tomatoes, and garnish in any of the following ways: with an olive slice, a strip of red or yellow pepper, a ring of tiny capers, or 1 or 2 parsley leaves. Serve at room temperature or slightly chilled.

FRESH BERRY RICE PUDDING PARFAITS

Prep time: **10 minutes** | Cook time: **45 minutes** | Serves **4–6**

- 2 cups whole milk
- 1 teaspoon vanilla extract
- 2 cups short-grain rice
- ⅓ cup whipping cream or panna di cucina
- 2 tablespoons honey
- ½ teaspoon cinnamon
- 2 cups mixed berries (blueberries, raspberries, blackberries)
- Whipped cream and mint leaves, for garnish

1. Heat the milk and vanilla extract in a medium saucepan over medium heat and bring to a boil. Add the rice and cook for about 15 minutes, stirring occasionally. Remove from the heat and add the whipping cream, honey, and cinnamon. Refrigerate, covered, for 30 minutes.

2. Assemble the parfaits in three layers: Using parfait cups, fill the bottom third of the cups with a layer of the pudding, fill the middle third with a layer of berries, then fill the top third with another layer of pudding. Garnish the top of each cup with a dollop of whipped cream, some more berries, and a mint leaf.

SPRITZ COCKTAIL

Prep time: **2 minutes** | Cook time: **none** | Serves **4**

- 12 ice cubes
- ⅔ cup Prosecco
- ⅔ cup Aperol
- ⅔ cup sparkling water or soda
- 8 orange slices

1. Add 2 or 3 ice cubes to each glass. Don't add too many or the drink will be a little too watered down when it melts.

2. Fill each glass one-third full with the Prosecco.

3. Add the Aperol, and top with the sparkling water.

4. Decorate with 1 or 2 orange slices.

MEASUREMENT CONVERSION CHART

VOLUME EQUIVALENTS(DRY)

US STANDARD	METRIC (APPROXIMATE)
1/8 teaspoon	0.5 mL
1/4 teaspoon	1 mL
1/2 teaspoon	2 mL
3/4 teaspoon	4 mL
1 teaspoon	5 mL
1 tablespoon	15 mL
1/4 cup	59 mL
1/2 cup	118 mL
3/4 cup	177 mL
1 cup	235 mL
2 cups	475 mL
3 cups	700 mL
4 cups	1 L

VOLUME EQUIVALENTS(LIQUID)

US STANDARD	US STANDARD (OUNCES)	METRIC (APPROXIMATE)
2 tablespoons	1 fl.oz.	30 mL
1/4 cup	2 fl.oz.	60 mL
1/2 cup	4 fl.oz.	120 mL
1 cup	8 fl.oz.	240 mL
1 1/2 cup	12 fl.oz.	355 mL
2 cups or 1 pint	16 fl.oz.	475 mL
4 cups or 1 quart	32 fl.oz.	1 L
1 gallon	128 fl.oz.	4 L

TEMPERATURES EQUIVALENTS

FAHRENHEIT(F)	CELSIUS(C) (APPROXIMATE)
225 °F	107 °C
250 °F	120 °C
275 °F	135 °C
300 °F	150 °C
325 °F	160 °C
350 °F	180 °C
375 °F	190 °C
400 °F	205 °C
425 °F	220 °C
450 °F	235 °C
475 °F	245 °C
500 °F	260 °C

WEIGHT EQUIVALENTS

US STANDARD	METRIC (APPROXIMATE)
1 ounce	28 g
2 ounces	57 g
5 ounces	142 g
10 ounces	284 g
15 ounces	425 g
16 ounces (1 pound)	455 g
1.5 pounds	680 g
2 pounds	907 g

APPENDIX 2: THE DIRTY DOZEN AND CLEAN FIFTEEN

The Dirty Dozen and Clean Fifteen

The Environmental Working Group (EWG) is a nonprofit, nonpartisan organization dedicated to protecting human health and the environment Its mission is to empower people to live healthier lives in a healthier environment. This organization publishes an annual list of the twelve kinds of produce, in sequence, that have the highest amount of pesticide residue-the Dirty Dozen-as well as a list of the fifteen kinds ofproduce that have the least amount of pesticide residue-the Clean Fifteen.

THE DIRTY DOZEN

- The 2016 Dirty Dozen includes the following produce. These are considered among the year's most important produce to buy organic:

Strawberries	Spinach
Apples	Tomatoes
Nectarines	Bell peppers
Peaches	Cherry tomatoes
Celery	Cucumbers
Grapes	Kale/collard greens
Cherries	Hot peppers

- *The Dirty Dozen list contains two additional itemskale/collard greens and hot peppers-because they tend to contain trace levels of highly hazardous pesticides.*

THE CLEAN FIFTEEN

- The least critical to buy organically are the Clean Fifteen list. The following are on the 2016 list:

Avocados	Papayas
Corn	Kiw
Pineapples	Eggplant
Cabbage	Honeydew
Sweet peas	Grapefruit
Onions	Cantaloupe
Asparagus	Cauliflower
Mangos	

- *Some of the sweet corn sold in the United States are made from genetically engineered (GE) seedstock. Buy organic varieties of these crops to avoid GE produce.*

93

Printed in Great Britain
by Amazon